Digital Painting
fundamentals
with
Corel® Painter® X3

Rhoda Draws

Cengage Learning PTR

CENGAGE
Learning·

Professional · Technical · Reference

Australia, Brazil, Japan, Korea, Mexico, Singapore, Spain, United Kingdom, United States

**Digital Painting Fundamentals
with Corel® Painter® X3**
Rhoda Draws

**Publisher and General Manager,
Cengage Learning PTR:**
Stacy L. Hiquet

Associate Director of Marketing:
Sarah Panella

Manager of Editorial Services:
Heather Talbot

Acquisitions Editor:
Heather Hurley

Project/Copy Editor:
Gill Editorial Services

Technical Reviewer:
Barbara Pollak

Interior Layout:
Shawn Morningstar

Cover Designer:
Mike Tanamachi

Proofreader /Indexer:
Kelly Talbot Editing Services

For product information and technology assistance,
contact us at
**Cengage Learning Customer & Sales Support,
1-800-354-9706.**

For permission to use material from this text or product,
submit all requests online at **cengage.com/permissions.**

Further permissions questions can be emailed to
permissionrequest@cengage.com.

Library of Congress Control Number: 2013947217
ISBN-13: 978-1-285-84069-7
ISBN-10: 1-285-84069-0

Cengage Learning PTR
20 Channel Center Street
Boston, MA 02210
USA

Cengage Learning is a leading provider of customized learning solutions
with office locations around the globe, including Singapore, the United
Kingdom, Australia, Mexico, Brazil, and Japan. Locate your local office
at: **international.cengage.com/region**

Cengage Learning products are represented in Canada by Nelson
Education, Ltd.

For your lifelong learning solutions, visit **cengageptr.com.**
Visit our corporate website at **cengage.com.**

Printed in the United States of America
1 2 3 4 5 6 7 15 14 13

For Stephen, Andy, Tanya, and all my Canadian colleagues and friends.

Acknowledgments

I'm grateful to publisher Stacy Hiquet and everyone at Cengage Learning for inviting me back to write a fourth edition of *Digital Painting Fundamentals with Corel Painter*. I want to thank Heather Hurley for overseeing everything and overlooking nothing. Huge thanks to Karen Gill, my project and copy editor, for her expertise and good humor. A big hug for Barbara Pollak, who earned another day at the spa for a great technical review. Shawn Morningstar did her usual fantastic layout design. A very special thank-you goes to Claudia Salguero for revealing the secrets of her urban illustration techniques in Lesson 10.

Thanks to all who donated their photos and likenesses to provide source images for the projects. Special thanks go to Jim McCartney and Doug Little at Wacom Technologies for continuing to raise the bar for pressure-sensitive graphics tablets and for sending me a new tablet every couple of years even though the old ones never break.

Finally, I am deeply grateful to Stephen Bolt, Andy Church, and Tanya Lux at Corel Corporation for including me in the Advisory Council for the development of the awesome new features and refinements in Painter X3.

About the Author

Rhoda Draws, the artist formerly known as Rhoda Grossman, is the author of numerous books and video tutorials on the creative uses of Corel Painter and Adobe Photoshop. She began to transfer her traditional fine art, illustration, and cartooning skills to the computer in the early 1990s. Based in the San Francisco Bay area, Rhoda draws and paints at Sausalito's historic Industrial Center Building (ICB), where she works in both digital and "messy" media. She uses a MacBook Pro and Wacom tablet in live sessions with a nude model, where she specializes in quick gesture drawings. Many of these sketches are printed on archival papers or combined into more complex images that inspire acrylic or mixed media work on canvas. Rhoda accepts portrait commissions in both pixels and pigment. Doing business as Rhoda Draws A Crowd, she creates live digital caricature entertainment for trade shows and corporate events. Visit her website at www.rhodadraws.com.

Contents

Part II Beyond the Basics

6

7

8

Introduction

Welcome to Corel Painter X3

You may pronounce it either *Ex Three* or *Thirteen*. However you say it, this is the fourth edition of *Digital Painting Fundamentals with Corel Painter*. So I guess we must be doing something right. This edition is even better than the earlier ones, and it's not just a coincidence that Corel Painter is better than ever, too. This book will get you started using Corel Painter. You will get step-by-step instruction for using the basic software and hardware that are the industry standard for pixel-based drawing and painting—Corel Painter and a Wacom graphics tablet. (If you're not sure what a tablet is or what pixels are, see the Appendix.) Exercises and projects will give you increasing control of tools and techniques. You will acquire and sharpen the skills needed for working in any medium, such as eye-hand coordination and drawing what you see. But there's more to digital art than just knowing how to make a series of marks on an electronic canvas—you will also be introduced to traditional art concepts dealing with composition, color, and style.

With Corel Painter, there's no need for the labor of stretching canvas and preparing a surface to accept pigment. You won't need to replenish dried-up tubes of paint or replace broken chalks and worn-out brushes. Your clothes won't get spattered with ink, you won't need to inhale toxic fumes, and your hands will stay clean. (For artists who would actually miss the messiness of a traditional studio, Wacom might be working on making a leaky pen that smells like turpentine!) You can save every version of a painting as it develops. Your digital paper won't wrinkle, your colors won't fade, and with 32 levels of **Undo**, there's no such thing as a mistake. As for storage space, hundreds of drawings and paintings can fit onto a tiny flash drive.

Historically Speaking

Unleashed in the early 1990s, Painter brought forth a new era for pixel-based digital graphics. Painter was the first Natural Media Emulation program, created for artists by artists! With this software, along with the newly developed pressure-sensitive graphics tablets to replace the mouse, artists could now begin to work comfortably at the computer. Painter has matured over the years and remains unrivaled for its capacity to imitate virtually any natural medium. It also has a considerable number of bells and whistles for creating effects that go way beyond what can be produced "naturally."

When Painter was released, I was in the right place at the right time (for a change), creating digital caricatures as a booth attraction for computer graphics trade shows. I painted with Photoshop then, but when I saw what Painter could do, I knew what my future looked like. I still rely on Photoshop for certain image manipulation tasks, but Photoshop's brush tool is anemic compared to Painter's robust array of brush styles and controls. Incidentally, these two apps have become more and more compatible with each other over the years. You can create an image in either program and then open it in the other for additional work, using the best features of each. Taken together, Photoshop and Painter are the Dream Team for pixel-pushers.

What's New?

Users of Painter 12 and earlier versions will find that Painter X3 introduces several great options for enhancing your productivity and work flow. New features include enhancements to cloning and a Reference Image panel. You can zoom, pan, and sample colors from the Reference Image while maintaining focus on your digital painting.

With nearly 1,000 separate brush variants to choose from, you will welcome the new **Brush Search** feature. Just type one or more descriptive words for brush behavior in the search field and up comes a list of all the brushes that satisfy your criteria. You can even create a custom palette directly from the **Brush Search** results! A new **Brush** category provides sophisticated Jitter settings.

Perspective guides are introduced in this version, as well as a handy way to transform more than one layer at a time. I'm delighted to see that there is now a way to limit the number of colors when creating a new color set.

How to Use This Book

Lessons 1, 2, and 3 (in that order) will give you enough of the fundamentals to get you up and running. After that, you can feel free to jump around and do what looks interesting at the moment. Within a lesson, it's a good idea to start with the first project and work down, but even that isn't absolutely required. Each lesson begins with a list of images and other items that will be needed for the projects. Download them in advance from the website that supports this book so you can find them quickly.

Be My PAL

Most of the resource files for this book are images, but there are a few files in .PAL format. These are custom palettes that can be opened only as follows: launch Painter and find the **Custom Palette Organizer** in the **Window** menu. Use the **Import** command, shown in Figure I.1, to find the .PAL file you have already downloaded to your hard drive. Please do that before you email me personally to complain that you can't open a .PAL file by double-clicking on it or using the **File > Open** command.

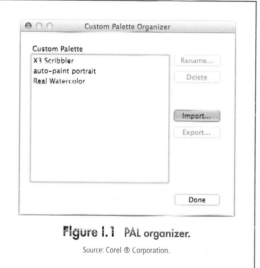

Figure I.1 PAL organizer.

Source: Corel ® Corporation.

Each project is liberally illustrated with images at various stages to keep you on track. Screen captures of dialog boxes, menus, or panels were made on a Mac, but the difference between them and the Windows version is merely cosmetic. In any case, I'll give keyboard commands for both Mac and PC. For example: **Command/Ctrl** means to use the **Command** key if you're on a Mac, the **Ctrl** key if you use Windows. Including the keystroke equivalent every time I mention a command will be awkward, so I added a list of the most popular keyboard shortcuts in the Appendix. A much more inclusive list is provided in Painter X3 **Preferences > Customize Keys**.

Users of previous versions will feel comfortable with Painter X3. You'll see a little NEW X3 icon pointing out new features as I introduce them. Photoshop users will find that a great many Painter tools, palettes, and commands are the same or similar to what they are accustomed to.

The Appendix provides some basic terms and definitions, along with other handy bits of information. There are resources for images, fonts, and printing and even a little free legal advice. So take a look back there once in a while.

Where Did I Leave That CD?

No need to worry—all the source images and other special items to help you work the projects are available on a website that supports this book: www.cengageptr.com/downloads. That's where you'll find images and custom palettes needed for the projects, organized by lesson number or by subject categories. There are photos of people, places, and things mostly shot by me. In addition to the specific images used in each lesson, many more photos are provided for you to choose from or to use in your own projects—just promise to use them for good and not for evil.

Corel Painter provides ways to organize your favorite tools and art materials. The **Pals&Libs** folder contains custom palettes and libraries to accompany specific projects, making it easier for you to jump right into a lesson without having to rummage around searching for the recommended items. Files ending in .PAL must be imported with the custom palette organizer, and files ending in .LIB must be loaded from the specific media panel: **Papers**, **Patterns**, **Gradients**, and so forth. Figure I.2 shows how to import an alternate paper library. You'll learn how easy it is to create your own custom palettes and libraries. I am providing fewer custom palettes in this edition, on the assumption that it's almost as easy for you to make your own, and that doing so will build your character and self-esteem.

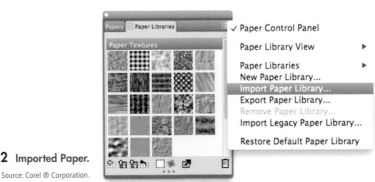

Figure I.2 Imported Paper.

Source: Corel ® Corporation.

The **Rhoda Portfolio** folder has samples of my digital art created in successive versions of Painter, spanning over 20 years. These show my use of several styles, showcasing the range and versatility of Painter. You'll see some illustration assignments as well as personal projects, portraits, abstract painting, cartooning, and experimental caricature created live at trade shows and other events.

But enough about me. I'll see you in Lesson 1.

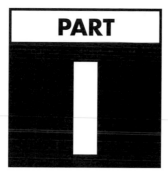

PART
I

The Basics

1 Let's Get Started

I believe in the power of creative scribbling. Painter will delight the inner scribbler in you! I made these marks with several of my favorite brush variants. Some of the strokes can be made with earlier versions of the program, but a few were done with new and exciting brushes introduced in Painter X3. You can actually create digital scribbles as good as this! So, turn on your computer, plug in your Wacom tablet, launch your Painter program, and let's get ready to scribble!

When you see the Welcome screen, shown in Figure 1.1, you have some choices to make. First, you can scroll through examples of Painter art created by many skilled Painter Masters. Before you choose to **Create a New Image**, notice some other options. **Brush Tracking**, under the **Set-Up** section, is an essential feature for adjusting your Wacom tablet to your unique touch. Click it now to get the panel shown in Figure 1.2. Make a long variable stroke that feels natural to you in the blank rectangle. The colorful squiggle gives Painter the pressure and speed data it needs to optimize the tablet for you. A typical stroke starts and ends with less pressure, and that's exactly what is showing here: smaller dots at the beginning and end of the stroke. This is also proof that your pressure-sensitive tablet is working properly.

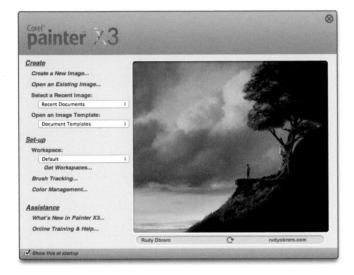

Figure 1.1 Wilkommen! Bienvenue! Welcome!
Source: Corel® Corporation.

Stay on Track

Painter remembers your touch even after you close and relaunch the program. You can access Brush Tracking any time using Painter's Preferences.

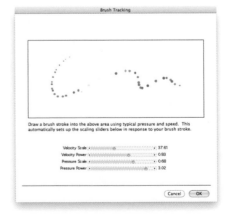

Figure 1.2 Take a stroke.
Source: Corel® Corporation.

The other items under **Set-Up** are **Workspace** (for customizing your Painter desktop) and **Color Management** (to optimize images for specific output devices). There's no need to deal with these choices just yet. The **Assistance** section has information about the new features and improvements in Painter X3. **Online Training & Help** can connect you with a wide range of video tutorials and other resources that are almost as good as this book.

Okay. Now you're ready to create an image. The New Image dialog box, shown in Figure 1.3, lets you enter height, width, and resolution for the canvas. We'll use 72 ppi most of the time, so you'll be able to see the whole canvas onscreen without scrolling, and you can work faster. (Pixels and resolution are explained in the Appendix, "Fundamentals and Beyond.") The default for **Color** is white unless you click the color swatch to change the canvas. **Basic Paper** is the default surface texture, but that tiny triangle at the lower right corner of the paper swatch lets you choose from several alternatives. If you want to reuse the same settings, click the plus sign next to the **Canvas Preset** field, and you'll be able to save the current configuration as a new preset. The minus sign indicates that you can remove presets you no longer need.

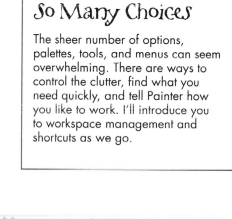

Figure 1.3 Choose size, resolution, color, and texture.
Source: Corel® Corporation.

So Many Choices

The sheer number of options, palettes, tools, and menus can seem overwhelming. There are ways to control the clutter, find what you need quickly, and tell Painter how you like to work. I'll introduce you to workspace management and shortcuts as we go.

I like to work on tinted paper for some projects, so I made a preset in the portrait orientation with a dusty rose color and rough charcoal paper. That preset is shown in Figure 1.4. This time I'm using pixels instead of inches. Of course, you may prefer to use centimeters as your unit, if you live anywhere in the world but the US of A.

Figure 1.4 Rough and ready for a rosy portrait.
Source: Corel® Corporation.

Gimme Some Space

The Painter **Workspace** consists of a combination of panels offering brushes and other art supplies as well as special features and commands. All panels are listed in the **Window** menu. You'll see the vertical **Toolbox** on the left side of your screen. I used Painter's **Preferences > Interface** to change the single column of tools into a double column—much easier for my eyes to scan. Choose the **Brush** tool, as shown in Figure 1.5. A tool or option is blue when it's active. If all you want to do is draw and paint, stick with the **Brush** tool; you can ignore most of the other choices in the **Toolbox** for a while.

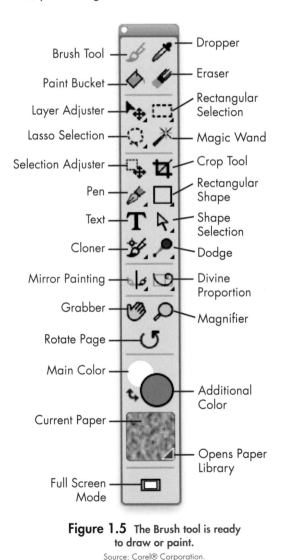

Figure 1.5 The Brush tool is ready to draw or paint.

Source: Corel® Corporation.

I'm still using the same trusty Intuos 4 medium-sized Wacom tablet that I had when writing the Painter 12 book two years ago. Figure 1.6 shows the basic grip ideal for most drawing and painting. You may want to disable the click functions on the side of your Wacom pen until you are ready to customize them. See the "Pick a Tablet" section in the Appendix for info on how to configure both your tablet and your pen. It's a good idea to check the support pages at Wacom. com to download the latest driver for whatever model tablet you're using. It looks like they provide continuing support for all tablets going nearly back to the Ten Commandments.

Pressure sensitivity enables you to control the width or opacity of your stroke by varying how hard you press the tip of the pen to the tablet as you work. Many of Painter's natural media brushes also respond to the tilt of your Wacom pen.

Figure 1.6 Same tablet, new bracelet.

© 2014 Cengage Learning.

The marks you make with your Wacom pen can imitate virtually any traditional art materials. You'll choose your digital brush with the **Brush Selector** in the upper-left corner of the Painter workspace. It has two main sections: one for the colorful icons representing each of 30 categories, and the other for the specific variant within the selected category. Below them is the **Dab and Stroke Preview**, showing a cross section of the brush tip and a sample stroke made with gray. Figure 1.7 shows that the **Calligraphy** variant of the **Pens** category is the current choice. The dab, or footprint, of the **Calligraphy** variant is like a thin blade at a 45-degree angle. It makes a thick line when used vertically and a thin line on the diagonal. Give it a try. My calligraphy skills are a bit rusty, as shown in Figure 1.8. You can see the **Dab and Stroke Preview** of any brush simply by "mousing" over it or hovering with your Wacom pen.

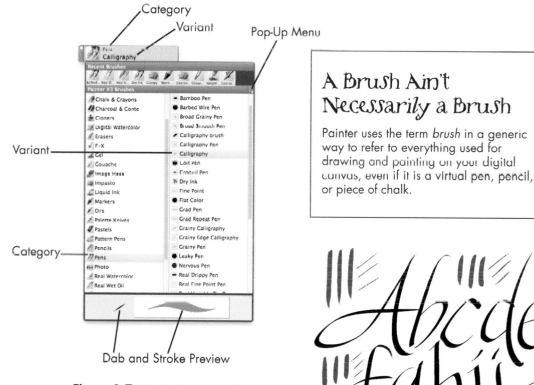

A Brush Ain't Necessarily a Brush

Painter uses the term *brush* in a generic way to refer to everything used for drawing and painting on your digital canvas, even if it is a virtual pen, pencil, or piece of chalk.

Figure 1.7 The Brush Selector shows the selected variant.

Source: Corel® Corporation.

Figure 1.8 Calligraphy.

© 2014 Cengage Learning.

I Love the Pressure!

Choose the **Dry Ink** variant in the **Pens** category and notice the **Dab and Stroke Preview**, shown in Figure 1.9. Make some strokes and squiggles with variations in the pressure on your Wacom tablet. **Dry Ink** is one of my favorite variants for drawing because of its juicy-looking bristles and extreme variations in line width based on pressure, as shown in Figure 1.10. Did your strokes respond to pressure variations? Even more important, did the lines appear where you wanted them? Use the "Test Your Tablet" note to confirm that your Wacom tablet is functioning properly. If pen strokes require more pressure than you're comfortable with, or (on the other hand) if the pen seems too sensitive to pressure changes, recall that you can customize the tablet's sensitivity within Painter by using **Preferences > Brush Tracking**.

Figure 1.9 A bristly dab.
Source: Corel® Corporation.

Figure 1.10 Through thick and thin.
© 2014 Cengage Learning.

Test Your Tablet

Make sure the tablet is mapped to your computer screen by doing the "two-point test." Touch the point of your Wacom pen to any corner of the active area of the tablet, and notice that your cursor shows up at the corresponding corner of your screen. That was one point. (If that didn't work, you're in trouble—see the "Pick a Tablet" section in the Appendix.) Now lift the pen away from the tablet (don't drag it!), and touch it to the opposite/diagonal corner. If the cursor shows up in the new position, you're good to go. If it doesn't, see the Appendix.

Finders and Keepers

Notice the horizontal strip of category icons called **Recent Brushes** in Figure 1.7. It is aptly named, allowing you to access any of the ten brush variants you used most recently. **Recent Brushes** are even remembered from your previous sessions. That's helpful if you want to avoid having to find a recently used brush by searching through the list of categories and variants.

Painter X3 introduces another way to find a brush, even if you haven't used it yet! The **Search Brushes** feature, shown in Figure 1.11, allows you to enter one or a combination of brush names or attributes. Then when you press **Enter** or **Return**, all brush variants that fit your search parameters appear in a drop-down list. Just click on one, and it becomes the active brush variant. The category name is indicated, and you have a **Dab and Stroke Preview** at the bottom of the list to help you choose.

Figure 1.11 Search me!
Source: Corel® Corporation.

Suppose you want to explore the new brushes introduced in Painter X3. They are easy to find: just type **X3** in the **Search** field, and you get the results shown in Figure 1.12. Maybe you remember part of the name of a variant, like "Soft Wet" something or "Grainy Hard" whatsit. Enter what you know in **Search Brushes**, and chances are you'll find several possibilites that will include what you're looking for.

Figure 1.12 A whole lotta Jitter goin' on.
Source: Corel® Corporation.

9

There are several ways to find a color to work with. The basic color picker is shown in Figure 1.13. Click or tap anywhere on the hue ring to choose a position on the color wheel, and then click inside the triangle for the **Value** (brightness) and **Saturation** (purity) you want. The **Color Set Libraries**, shown in Figure 1.14, allow you to load a limited set of colors or create a new set customized for a specific project or style.

Figure 1.13 All possible colors.
Source: Corel® Corporation.

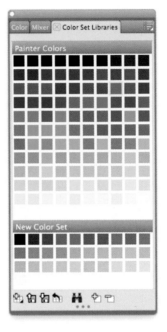

Figure 1.14 Custom colors.
Source: Corel® Corporation.

Let's Doodle

Make a new canvas big enough to fill your screen at 100% size. Try out some **Pencils, Markers,** and **Pastels**. (Pastels are like chalk, only much more expensive.) Choose **Square Hard Pastel** from the **Pastels** category, and notice the **Dab and Stroke Preview**, as shown in Figure 1.15. The strokes shown in Figure 1.16 were made with different paper textures, showing how well this variant imitates the response to paper grain of traditional pastel sticks. Painter brush variants that show paper grain usually have the term *grainy* in their name. Increasing tablet pressure does not make this stroke wider, but more opaque. Going over the stroke again increases opacity and eventually fills in the paper grain. Light colors of chalk and pastels can cover darker ones. By contrast, overlapping marker strokes build up, getting darker and denser. Painter uses the terms *cover* and *buildup* to describe these two basic methods for determining the behavior of a brush variant.

Figure 1.15 Rectangular dab.
Source: Corel® Corporation.

You'll find the current library of paper textures at the bottom of the **Toolbox**. Just click the little blue triangle to open it, and select any texture you want. I made the top stroke in Figure 1.16 with **Basic Paper**. Then I switched to **Coarse Cotton Canvas**, and finally **Pebble Board**.

Figure 1.16 Grainy strokes.
© 2014 Cengage Learning.

Brush Ghosting

As your Wacom pen hovers over the canvas, you may want to see the "ghost" of the dab between strokes. There are a few other choices for the cursor, available in the **Preferences > Interface** panel shown in Figure 1.17. **Enhanced Brush Ghost** shows you the angle of your Wacom pen (as if you didn't know!) and can result in performance lags for some brushes.

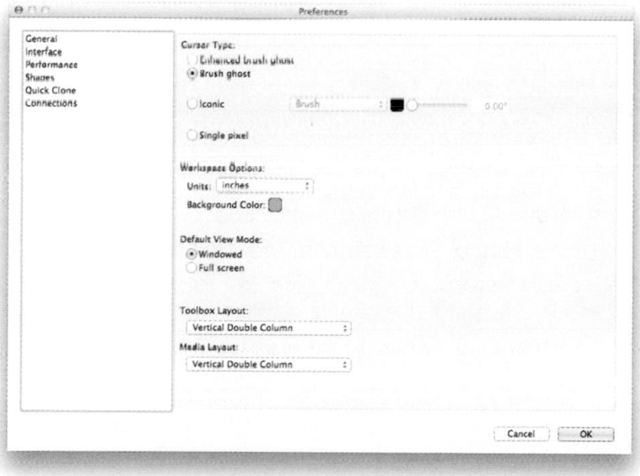

Figure 1.17 Interface Preferences.
Source: Corel® Corporation.

Let's Get Real

Seems like only yesterday that Painter 11 (eleven!) introduced a group of **"Real"** brush variants with enhanced capabilities to emulate natural media. Choose **Real 6B Soft Pencil** and a dark gray color. The marks you make with the Wacom pen held upright are thin lines, but as you tilt your pen, the lines become wider. You can make a very wide stroke if you change your grip so that the pen is at a steep angle, as shown in Figure 1.18. This imitates shading with the side of a pencil or pigment stick.

Figure 1.18 The Side stroke.
© 2014 Cengage Learning.

Traditional paintbrushes are composed of numerous bristles that can range in length, thickness, and stiffness. The kind of mark made by a bristle brush depends on a large number of factors: quality and number of bristles, viscosity and amount of paint loaded, and pressure and direction of the artist's stroke. There are several Painter categories devoted to bristle-type brushes. They include **Acrylics**, **Oils**, and **Impasto** (Italian for *thick paint*). Take a couple of variants from each of those categories for a test drive. The following variants made the strokes shown in Figure 1.19.

Acrylic: Thick Acrylic Bristle

Oils: Coarse Wet Bristle

Artists: Van Gogh

As expected, the **Acrylic** variant looks thick, while the **Oil** brush really seems wet. The **Van Gogh** variant is not a bristle brush, but a Rake type. It has parallel striations, with color variability among the strands. **Van Gogh** is most effective when applied in short strokes, because of randomness built into the color variation. Each time you make a fresh mark, the color variability is reset.

Figure 1.19 Thick, Wet, and Rakish.
© 2014 Cengage Learning.

So Many Choices!

Every version of Painter introduces exciting new brushes or even whole new categories. Painter X3 brings us a group of brushes that incorporate an advanced Jitter feature. This variable has nothing to do with how much caffeine you have in your system. Categories may come and go, while familiar variants may have migrated to different categories. Any way you slice and dice the categories, there are nearly a thousand variants to choose from! Just exploring a fraction of them and keeping track of the ones you like can be a challenge. Fortunately, there are ways to organize brushes and other items, so you can quickly find the ones you need for a project.

If you prefer to work with a brush library from a previous version of Painter, you can. Switch Brush Libraries in the **Brush Selector** drop-down menu, as shown in Figure 1.20. The check mark shows that Painter X3 brushes are currently loaded, but you can replace them with the Brush Library from either v. 11 or 12. Notice some of the other choices available in this menu. I have unchecked **Recent Brushes** and the **Dab and Stroke Preview** to hide them and save valuable desktop real estate. I also chose to display the categories as large icons instead of by name.

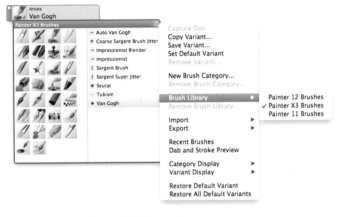

Figure 1.20 Brush Selector menu.

Source: Corel® Corporation.

Custom Palettes

After you've been working with Painter for a while, you'll probably have some favorite brushes, paper textures, and other bits and pieces. You can collect them in one or more compact little palettes that you can use over and over. Custom palettes are easy to make. Choose a brush variant you want, and press the **Shift** key while you drag the brush icon away from the **Brush Selector**. A new custom palette is created containing that variant. Add more brushes, papers, gradients, patterns, and so on by simply **Shift**-dragging in more items. Hold down the **Shift** key to remove or reposition items within the custom palette. Figure 1.21 shows the first two items in a custom palette: **Dry Ink** from the **Pens** category and **Chunky Oil Pastel**. Hovering or rolling over an item in the custom palette reveals the color of the category icon and shows the name of the variant. Custom palettes are suggested for many of the lessons. I will give you a list of brushes you need at the beginning of each project, and you can make your own custom palette.

Figure 1.21 Dry and chunky.

Source: Corel® Corporation.

Meanwhile, Back at the Palettes

Create a different custom palette for sketching, painting, working with photos, or any special project. Manage them with the **Custom Palette Organizer**, shown in Figure 1.22, by choosing **Window > Custom Palette > Organizer**. Give them descriptive names and save them using the **Export** command. Load them with the **Import** command.

Figure 1.22 Get organized.
Source: Corel® Corporation.

Back to the Drawing Board

Your first assignment is to fill a blank canvas with scribbles and strokes, using the 13 brushes in a custom palette shown in Figure 1.23. Download the **Painter X3 Scribbler** palette from the website that supports this book. Or just make it from scratch, using the following list, where the category is followed by the variant.

Top Row:

- Gel > Gel Fractal Jitter
- Airbrushes > Course Spray Jitter
- Artists > Sargent Super Jitter
- Gouache > Gouache Rake Jitter
- Impasto > Course Impasto Jitter

Second Row:

- Oils > Coarse Wet Bristle
- Artists > Coarse Sargent Brush Jitter
- Oils > Dense Impasto Block Jitter

Third Row:

- Pencils > Real 6B Soft Pencil
- Pens > Barbed Wire Pen
- Pens > Dry Ink
- Impasto > Gloopy
- Markers > Worn Marker Jitter

Figure 1.23
The Scribbler palette.
Source: Corel® Corporation.

Scribble a Sampler

Just because your main purpose is to become familiar with brushes doesn't mean your work can't look good. To help make something more pleasing to the eye, restrict yourself to one color or family of colors. A limited color palette tends to create visual harmony even with lots of variety in brush strokes, texture, and detail. You may change the saturation and brightness of the main color by clicking in the triangle of the **Color Panel**, but stick with the same position on the **Hue** ring. Consider grouping your scribbles to make a composition based on shapes or other variables. My sampler is shown in Figure 1.24.

Figure 1.24 My sampler.
© 2014 Cengage Learning.

Did some of the brush variants surprise you? Which ones do you want to use again? Did you notice that a few of the variants in the custom palette share the same icon? That's because they are in the same category. **Barbed Wire Pen** and **Dry Ink** are both from the **Pens** category. You can remember which is which by their position, but it's easy to replace the category icon with a more distinctive custom image. Let's make one for the **Barbed Wire Pen**.

Find an area in your sampler that was made with the **Barbed Wire Pen**, or just make a new squiggle with it. Choose the **Rectangular Selection** tool in the **Toolbox**, and drag it to enclose a small section of the **Barbed Wire** stroke, as shown in Figure 1.25. Click on the **Barbed Wire** variant in the custom palette, and right-click (that's **Ctrl-click** for Mac users) to bring up the menu shown in Figure 1.26. Choose the **Capture Custom Icon** command; the result is some lovely red wires in place of the Pens icon, as shown in Figure 1.27.

Figure 1.25 Cutting the wires.
© 2014 Cengage Learning.

Figure 1.26 Getting your wires crossed.
Source: Corel® Corporation.

Proceed at Your Own Risk!

Explore other brush categories now, or any time, but be warned—some of them are exotic, to say the least. For example, **Pattern Pens** don't apply the current color, but paint with the current pattern. (You'll find that library right under **Papers** at the bottom of the **Toolbox**.) **Watercolor** and **Real Watercolor** brushes require a special layer, created automatically when you use them. **Liquid Ink** is in a class (and layer) by itself. As for the **Image Hose**—don't get me started!

Figure 1.27 Live wires.
Source: Corel® Corporation.

Control Yourself

Here are some exercises for developing skill with the Wacom tablet. Use them as a warm-up before you begin a session and to check whether you need to reset the **Brush Tracker** for your pressure and speed.

Crosshatching

Start with a new white canvas about 900 pixels square. Choose **Pen > Ball Point Pen**, and use black as the main color. Refer to Figure 1.28 as you work. Make a long mark at the angle natural for you. I'm right-handed, so my strokes will slant slightly to the left. There is no width variation in this pen, just like its real-world counterpart. Your second stroke should be parallel to the first and reasonably close to it. Add several more strokes the same distance apart. Go for accuracy the first few times, and then increase your speed.

Figure 1.28 Hatch and crosshatch.
© 2014 Cengage Learning.

Next, use the **Rotate Page** tool and make another series of lines at right angles to the first set. After that, tilt the page so you can add lines at a 45-degree angle. You can probably guess the next step. The crosshatching skill will come in handy when you want to develop shading and volume in drawings.

Pressure Practice

Make a new canvas for the next exercise or simply clear this one, using **Select All (Cmd/Ctrl+A)** followed by **Delete/Backspace**. Switch to the **Dry Ink** brush, which was used in your sampler painting. This is the ideal variant for practicing pressure control. Make a long stroke that begins with light pen pressure, gradually increase pressure to the maximum width, and then taper off as you end the stroke. It might take several tries to get the right touch for a smooth transition. Check out the practice strokes in Figure 1.29.

Sensitivity Training

Making smooth transitions in line width will be easier if you are using a Wacom tablet with greater pressure sensitivity. The Intuos models have 2048 levels, and the Bamboo series offers "only" 1,024 levels. Fewer levels of pressure make it even more important to tweak the settings in **Preferences > Brush Tracking**.

Figure 1.29 Ink under pressure.
© 2014 Cengage Learning.

What's Next?

You're off to a good start. You have a basic understanding of how to choose and organize Painter brushes and how to show your Wacom tablet who's boss. In the following lessons, you'll practice skills and learn concepts for improving your mastery of drawing and painting. I promise to take you way beyond scribbling!

2 What U C Is What U Draw

Y ou'll begin with a simple subject and practice drawing it using different methods. First, you'll just create the outline. Then you'll add shading and color. Each new technique will teach you more about how to draw and how to use Painter X3.

For this lesson you'll use

- **Images:** lemon.jpg, mandarin_oranges.jpg, oranges.jpg

- **Custom palettes:** basic_drawing.pal

A Lemon a Day

One of the best assignments I ever had in a traditional art class was to create a series of 20 versions of an apple, each using a different medium or style. We worked with apples in the Painter 12 edition, after drawing pears in previous books. This time we'll get some fresh citrus fruit to pose for us. Open **lemon.jpg**, shown in Figure 2.1.

Figure 2.1 When life hands you lemons…

© 2014 Cengage Learning.

Size Matters

You may want to change the size of the lemon image to fit your screen. **Canvas > Resize** brings up the dialog box shown in Figure 2.2. Before you enter the new height or width, be sure to disable **Constrain File Size**. If you don't, the change in dimensions will be compensated with a change in resolution, and the image will be exactly the same size onscreen!

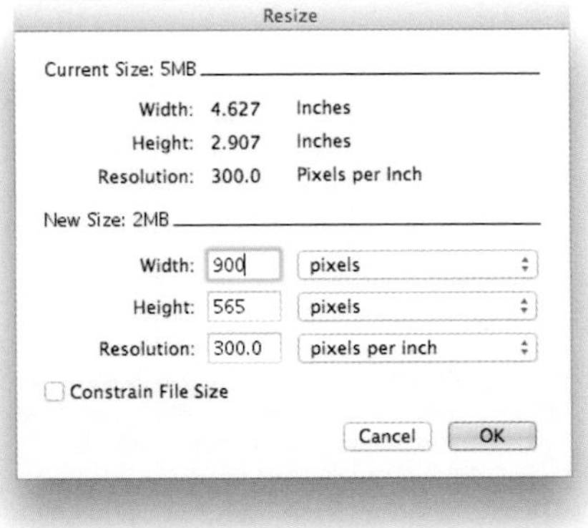

Figure 2.2 Your file size may vary.

Source: Corel ® Corporation.

Lemon Aid

The easiest way to draw an outline of the lemon is to trace it. The way to set up Painter's tracing function is with the **File > Quick Clone** command. **Quick Clone** automatically creates an exact copy of the lemon and deletes the image to give you a blank canvas. You will see a "ghost" of the original lemon, however, because **Tracing Paper** is on. The **Clone Source** panel, shown in Figure 2.3, has a slider to adjust the transparency of **Tracing Paper** and a toggle for turning **Tracing Paper** on or off as your drawing develops. A keystroke shortcut for the **Tracing Paper** toggle is **Cmd/Ctrl+T**. The original image will stay open if you choose the **Show Source Image** option in the **Clone Source** panel.

Use **Window > Custom Palette > Organizer** to import **basic_drawing.pal**, shown in Figure 2.4. (If you haven't already downloaded it from the website that supports this book, you can make this custom palette from scratch, using the variant names shown.) When your stylus hovers over an item in a custom palette, the icon appears in full color and a "tooltip" shows you the name of the variant.

Tracing Paper Toggle

Figure 2.3 An image source and vitamin C source.

Source: Corel ® Corporation.

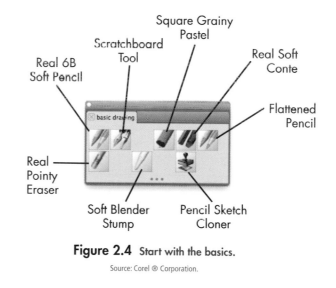

Figure 2.4 Start with the basics.

Source: Corel ® Corporation.

It's Been Real

Dry media (chalk, pencils, conte sticks, and pastels) that have the word "Real" in their names are capable of behaving in a realistic way when you tilt your stylus. Working with traditional dry media, you can make very wide marks when you hold the stick or pencil at an extreme angle. Figure 2.5 shows several strokes made with the **Real 6B Soft Pencil**, using black with the stylus held upright for a thin stroke and at various angles for broad lines. You can even change your grip to hold the stylus nearly parallel to the tablet, as shown in Figure 2.6, for the widest stroke possible —like drawing with the side of a piece of chalk!

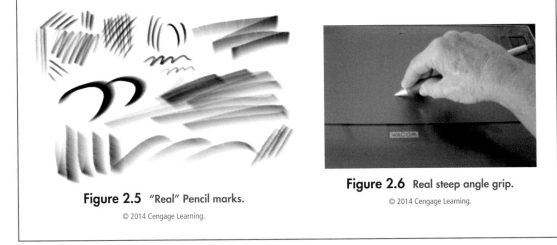

Figure 2.5 "Real" Pencil marks.

© 2014 Cengage Learning.

Figure 2.6 Real steep angle grip.

© 2014 Cengage Learning.

Pick a dark brown as your primary color and choose **Flattened Pencil** from the custom palette. You're ready to trace. Include an outline of the cast shadow. This **Pencil** variant doesn't have much thick-to-thin variation when you apply pressure. You can clean up the edges of your outline with the **Pointy Eraser**, but don't even try to be perfect. Figure 2.7 shows my effort. Don't forget to turn off **Tracing Paper** to see your drawing.

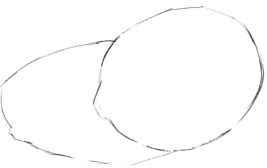

Figure 2.7 A trace of lemon.

© 2014 Cengage Learning.

Lemon Filling

You won't need **Tracing Paper** to fill in the outline with color. You can keep the lemon photo open as a reference, but Painter X3 offers a neat way to use any image as a reference without actually opening the file. Under the **Window** menu, find **Reference Image** about two-thirds of the way down. In the blank box that comes up, use the **Open Reference Image** command and navigate to the original **lemon.jpg** photo, as shown in Figure 2.8. You can zoom in or out with the **Magnifier** tool and move the image around with the **Grabber Hand**. Change the size of the box by dragging in or out from a corner or an edge. Most useful is the **Dropper** tool, to sample color anywhere on the image. That color now becomes Painter's main color, and you're ready to apply it to your drawing with the **Square Grainy Pastel**. Figure 2.9 shows my first few pastel strokes with colors sampled from the Reference Image.

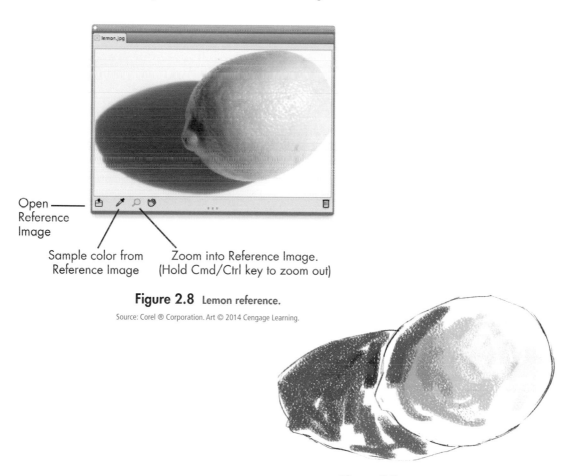

Open Reference Image

Sample color from Reference Image

Zoom into Reference Image. (Hold Cmd/Ctrl key to zoom out)

Figure 2.8 Lemon reference.

Source: Corel ® Corporation. Art © 2014 Cengage Learning.

Figure 2.9 Lemony samples.

© 2014 Cengage Learning.

Toggle Your Dropper

You don't need the Reference Image to sample a color. There is a **Dropper** tool in the main **Toolbox**. A speedy way to access it is to hold down the **Option/Alt** key while you are working. This changes your brush tool to the **Dropper** so you can tap your stylus on any desired color in your image. Release the modifier key, and your brush tool is back.

The *grainy* nature of the pastel stick means that it will show the current paper texture, which is the default **Basic Paper**. Let's find another texture that will imitate the skin of the lemon a bit better. Open **Paper** panels from the **Window** menu and notice that there are two tabs sharing the panel, shown in Figure 2.10. One section shows swatches for all the available textures in the current library. The other has an enlarged swatch with sliders for changing the size of the grain as well as its contrast and brightness.

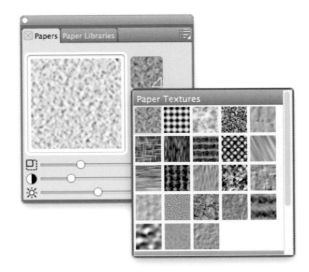

Figure 2.10 Swatches and sliders.

Source: Corel ® Corporation.

Papers, Please!

You could have opened the current paper library by clicking the little blue triangle in the **Paper** swatch at the bottom of the **Toolbox**. The reason we need to get **Papers** from the **Window** menu this time is to have access to the **Paper** controls.

Choose **Pebble Board**, the swatch in the lower-left corner of the library. Make some strokes on your drawing with **Hard Grainy Pastel**. Follow the contours of the fruit as you apply color. This texture seems close to the skin of our lemon, but it could use some tweaking in the **Papers** panel. To make the texture finer and more subtle, reduce the scale (size) and contrast, but increase the brightness. Figure 2.11 shows my settings, and Figure 2.12 compares **Basic Paper** with **Pebble Board** before and after adjustments.

Paper Scale
Paper Contrast
Paper Brightness

Figure 2.11 Finer pebbles.

Source: Corel ® Corporation.

Figure 2.12 Texture test.

© 2014 Cengage Learning.

The cast shadow is smooth, so use **Basic Paper** for that. To make switching swatches easy, add these two papers to your custom palette. Just hold the **Shift** key down and drag a paper swatch to the custom palette. A custom palette can also contain commands. The **Iterative Save** command in the **File** menu is a quick way to save the stages in the development of your pastel drawing. Add the **Iterative Save** command using **Window > Custom Palette > Add Command**. Be sure to specify that the command should be added to your basic_drawing.pal custom palette, as shown in Figure 2.13. Figure 2.14 shows the custom palette with paper swatches and the new command added.

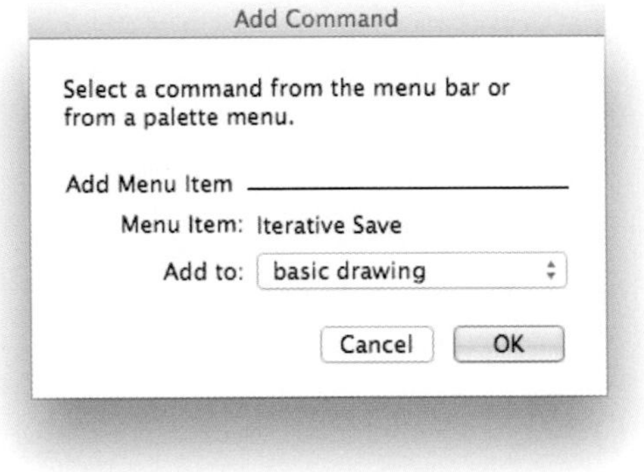

Figure 2.13 Basic command.

Source: Corel ® Corporation.

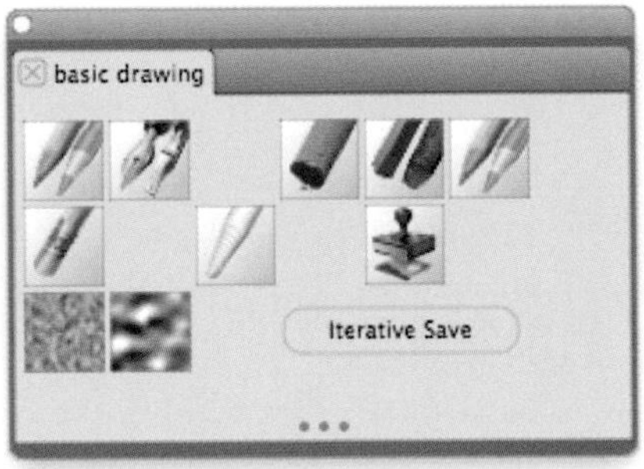

Figure 2.14 Custom alterations.

Source: Corel ® Corporation.

Continue to develop your pastel drawing of the lemon, using **Square Grainy Pastel** and the **Dropper** tool in the Reference Image to change color as needed. You can choose colors in the usual way, too. For smaller areas, use the **Real Soft Conte** stick. Smooth out the cast shadow with the **Soft Blender Stump** and use the **Real Pointy Eraser** to clean up edges.

Figure 2.15 shows a couple of stages in my drawing along with the finished work. For some natural-looking variations in the texture, I inverted the paper grain for some strokes. That means making a negative of the grayscale swatch that defines texture. Refer to Figure 2.11 again to see the not-so-obvious invert icon. Figure 2.16 shows how useful this can be, especially for creating two-tone effects.

Figure 2.15 Juicy subject.

© 2014 Cengage Learning.

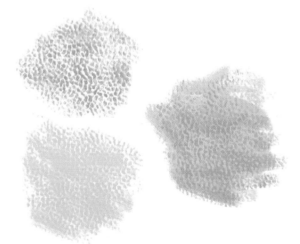

Figure 2.16 Paper inversion.

© 2014 Cengage Learning.

Love for Two Oranges

Open the **mandarin_oranges.jpg** image, shown in Figure 2.17. Resize it, if needed, to fit your screen. Make a **Quick Clone**.

Painter's cloning features are capable of much more than providing a way to trace an image. With **Cloner** brushes, you can turn photos into drawings or paintings in *virtually* any style, one brush stroke at a time. You saw how easy it was to find a color using the **Dropper** tool in a Reference Image. **Cloner** brushes apply exactly the right color automatically!

Figure 2.17 Nothing rhymes with "orange."

© 2014 Cengage Learning.

Drawing or Painting?

What's the difference between the two? Sometimes not much, and we may use these terms interchangeably. In general, drawings are made with dry media, and paintings with wet. Or, if you render your subject mostly with lines, it's a drawing. But when tones and colors blend into each other without distinct edges, it's a painting. A traditional term for artwork composed with a variety of wet and dry materials, possibly incorporating photos or collage elements pasted on, is *mixed media*. Technically, everything you make in Painter is *painting* because it's done with pixels. Digital *drawing* requires a vector-based program like Illustrator. I'm glad I could clear that up.

Painter provides a category devoted to **Cloner** brushes. The custom palette you've been using includes one, indicated by the rubber stamp icon. Any variant from any category can become a **Cloner**. Simply engage the **Rubber Stamp** icon in the **Color** panel. The hue ring and inner triangle will turn gray, as shown in Figure 2.18, indicating that you cannot pick colors. That choice is taken out of your hands. Choose the **Square Grainy Pastel** variant from the custom palette and engage **Clone** color. Check that you still have **Pebble Board** paper selected. Make several loose, rapid strokes on the blank image, following the rounded contours of the fruit. Increase the opacity of the **Tracing Paper** as needed. Figure 2.19 shows my first scribbly strokes, with **Tracing Paper** opacity turned up to 70%. After establishing the basic shapes, you can toggle **Tracing Paper** off.

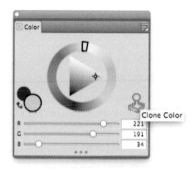

Figure 2.18 Gray and proud.

Source: Corel ® Corporation.

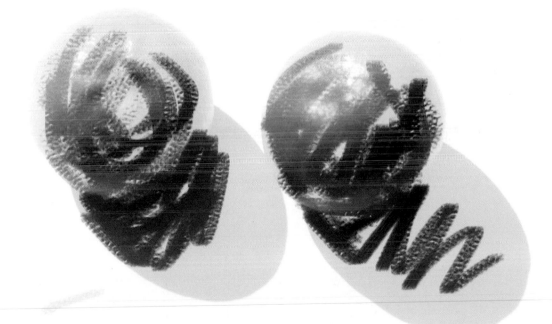

Figure 2.19 Loose and juicy.

© 2014 Cengage Learning.

Continue drawing with **Clone** color, but don't fill in too much. Traditional pastel drawings tend to allow some bits of paper to show through. To bring out some details, you need a smaller brush. The **Pencil Sketch Cloner** in your custom palette will work nicely. Figure 2.20 shows the finished drawing.

Figure 2.20 Orange appeal.

© 2014 Cengage Learning.

Cheaper by the Dozen

You'll explore more cloning techniques along with other Painter features, using the **oranges.jpg** image shown in Figure 2.21.

Figure 2.21 California oranges.

© 2014 Cengage Learning.

Make a **Quick Clone** of the **oranges.jpg** photo. You'll begin your drawing with black, using the **Scratchboard Tool** in your custom palette. This is an excellent **Pen** variant that produces smooth lines with a moderate amount of variation in width based on pressure. With **Tracing Paper** at the default 50% opacity, roughly sketch in only the darkest lines and shadow areas. Your work may look similar to Figure 2.22.

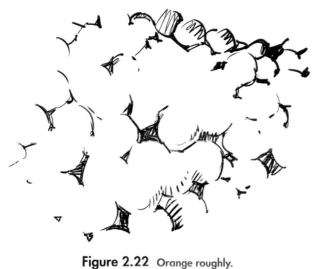

Figure 2.22 Orange roughly.

© 2014 Cengage Learning.

You Can Save That Again!

Get into the habit of using **Iterative Save**. The best way is to add the command to every custom palette you make. Or learn the three-fingered keystroke shortcut **Shift+Cmd/Ctrl+S**. This is useful for documenting the stages in a project. Better yet, you can go back in virtual time and redo a painting differently.

You can toggle **Tracing Paper** off at this point, because the black lines serve to guide you for the following stages. Choose **Square Hard Pastel** once again, and make sure that it is in **Clone Color** mode. Find another texture in the Paper library, such as French Watercolor paper. Add cloned strokes to some of the oranges, avoiding the black lines as much as you can, as shown in Figure 2.23.

Figure 2.23 Fruit filling.

© 2014 Cengage Learning.

Cheap Color Effects

Is the original Clone source image (**oranges.jpg**) open? If it's not, use the **Open Source Image** icon at the bottom of the **Clone Source** panel. To add some color variation to your artwork, you'll change the color scheme of the original **oranges.jpg** image. Find the **Underpainting** panel in the **Windows > Autopainting** panels. Choose **Impresssionist Scheme** in the **Color Scheme** field, as shown in Figure 2.24. As long as you're up, check out the different looks you can get with half a dozen color schemes available in the list. Figure 2.25 shows the difference between the original photo and the color-adjusted version.

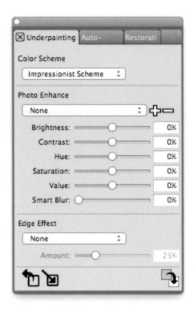

Figure 2.24 California scheming.

Source: Corel ® Corporation.

Figure 2.25 First Impressionist.

© 2014 Cengage Learning.

Use **File > Save As** to give your new version of the photo a descriptive name. In the **Clone Source** panel, use the **Open Source Image** command in the lower left to designate your color-enhanced photo as an additional clone source. As shown in Figure 2.26, you can now easily switch between the two clone sources as you develop your drawing.

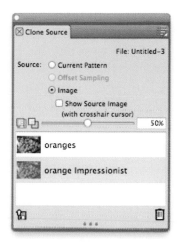

Figure 2.26 Orange, more or less.

Source: Corel ® Corporation. Art © 2014 Cengage Learning.

Proceed With or Without Caution

Painter X3 introduces a new feature designed to manage changes that you make in the Clone source image. When the "How do you want to proceed" dialog, shown in Figure 2.27, comes up you have an opportunity to either create a second source image, while leaving the original intact, or save changes to the original. The third option is basically "forget about it, just undo the changes, 'cause I can't decide."

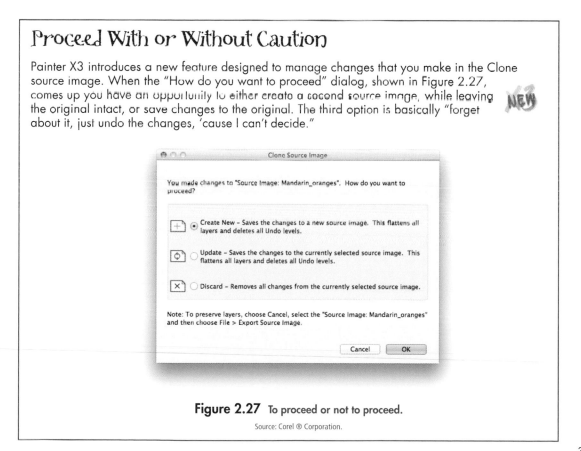

Figure 2.27 To proceed or not to proceed.

Source: Corel ® Corporation.

Use the color-enhanced clone source to fill in some of the oranges on the left and the upper right. Figure 2.28 shows that stage in my work. To make thinner strokes that bring out some detail, use either **Real Soft Conte** (be sure to enable **Clone color!**) or the **Pencil Sketch Cloner**. Smooth a few areas here and there with the **Soft Blender Stump**.

Figure 2.28 Ripening nicely.

Source: Corel ® Corporation.

Is It Done Yet?

A challenge in both traditional and digital painting is deciding when the work is finished. If your piece is an assignment for a client, it's done when the client is satisfied. If not, it's done when *you* are satisfied. Or it could be done when you've run out of time, or when you've lost interest in the project. I'm pretty happy with this piece, because it has a variety of textures and tonality, includes smooth and rough areas, and leaves a bit to the imagination. By that, I mean that details are literally "sketchy."

To Clone or Not to Clone?

You don't have to stick with Clone Color for the entire painting. Switch to picking color in the usual way whenever you want to, or use the Dropper to sample an existing color in the image. I did that to add the blue-green and muted purples to the lower corners of the finished drawing, shown in Figure 2.29.

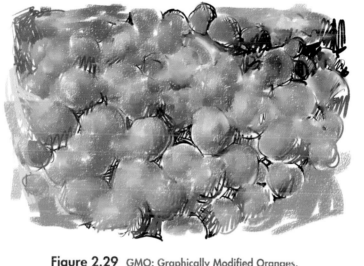

Figure 2.29 GMO: Graphically Modified Oranges.

© 2014 Cengage Learning.

What's Next?

You've had a brief introduction to the Painter environment. Practice using these tools and techniques to increase your skills. There are source photos on the website that supports this book to serve as subjects for drawing and painting. I also encourage you to go to the market and buy some nice fresh produce to work with. Make your own photos. Even better, set your hand-picked fruit or vegetable on a surface next to your computer and draw it live! Aim a spotlight on one side to get dramatic highlights and shadows.

After every lesson or practice session, choose your best couple of drawings and print them. That way you'll have tangible evidence of your work to hang on the walls. Over time you'll be able to observe your skills improving. Examining a print of your drawing is also a good way to evaluate it for possible changes. Most desktop inkjet printers can create high-quality output. To enhance the fine art nature of your image, use special paper or other media designed for your printer. High gloss heavyweight photo paper might be ideal for some projects, canvas or watercolor paper for others. (See the Appendix, "Fundamentals and Beyond," for resources.)

3 Take a Layer

Regardless of subject matter or style, it's often a good idea to separate elements of your artwork into layers. For example, draw outlines on one layer and create color on another. You'll be able to make changes to one layer while other layers are protected. You can even shuffle layers around to experiment with alternate compositions and effects.

For this lesson you'll use

- **Images:** market_basket.jpg, personal_pepperoni.jpg, cupcake_rack.jpg

- **Custom palettes:** basic_drawing.pal, cupcake_cloners.pal

Starter Still Life

For this project, you'll switch from fruit to vegetables. This will allow you to practice using the Painter tools and techniques you've been working with, and explore a few more. Plus, you'll get a whole diferent set of vitamins and minerals. Open **market_basket.jpg**, shown in Figure 3.1.

Figure 3.1 Farmers' market basket.

© 2014 Cengage Learning.

Basket of Goodness

You could use a bit more space at the top and bottom of the image, to allow your brush strokes to extend beyond the edges. Use **Canvas > Canvas Size** to add about 50 pixels above and below the photo, as shown in Figure 3.2.

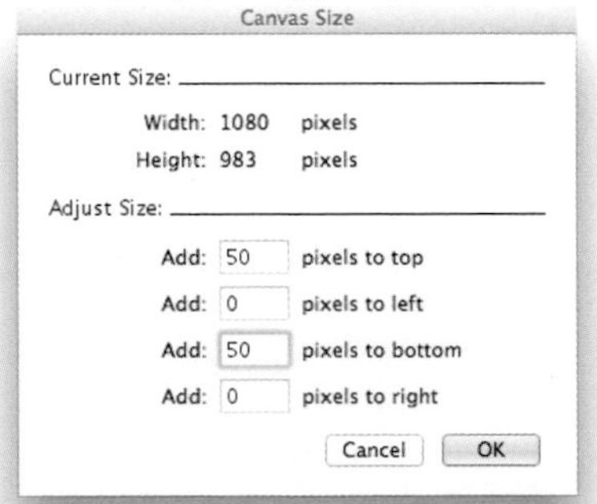

Figure 3.2 Gimme some space.

Source: Corel ® Corporation.

Use **File > Quick Clone** to access **Tracing Paper**. Choose **Real 6B Soft Pencil** from the custom palette and work with a dark brown or maroon color. Create a rough sketch that includes the basic shapes, tones, and textures, similar to my effort in Figure 3.3. You will probably need to tilt your drawing to sketch some areas more comfortably. Use the **Rotate Page** tool, found near the bottom of the **Toolbox**, under the **Magnifier**. Figure 3.4 shows my work tilted, with **Tracing Paper** at about 70% to reveal more of the drawing and less of the photo.

Figure 3.3 Sketchy veggies.

© 2014 Cengage Learning.

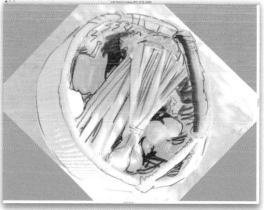

Figure 3.4 A real page turner.

Source: Corel ® Corporation. Art © 2014 Cengage Learning.

Not So Dark Shadows

Real 2B Soft Pencil is one of the versatile variants that can produce realistic shading when you hold your Wacom pen at a very steep angle. With a little practice, you can make wide strokes that also vary in opacity. Refer to Figure 1.18 in Lesson 1 to see a suggested grip for creating these results.

Colored Greens

You will add color to your sketch on a separate layer, protecting the work you did so far. Open the **Layers** panel, found in the **Window** menu. Click the **New Layer** icon at the botton of the panel to get the result shown in Figure 3.5.

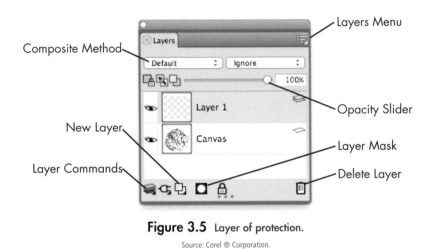

Figure 3.5 Layer of protection.

Source: Corel ® Corporation.

Dismiss the **Clone Source** panel and close the original photo if it is still in your workspace. You will paint the color freehand, using the photo only for reference. So, open the **Reference Image** panel and load the market basket photo. Ready to use a more sophisticated brush than the ones provided in the basic drawing palette? The **Real Clumpy Broad Bristle** brush in the **Oils** category has a juicy and smeary quality that can produce wonderful wet-into-wet effects, as shown in Figure 3.6. This brush also uses the Cover method, meaning you can paint light colors over dark, as in traditional oil media. Start a new custom palette with this brush, using the **Search** feature in Painter X3. Enter **real clumpy** in the search field and press **Enter/Return**. Only one variant fits this description, and it's the one you want. **Shift**-and-drag it from the search results, and it willl automatically make a new custom palette. If you drag it into your existing custom palette, it will find a spot for itself there.

Figure 3.6 Clumpy, broad, bristly, and real.

© 2014 Cengage Learning.

Apply colors sampled from the **Reference Image** to your new layer with
the **Real Clumpy Broad Bristle** brush. Your strokes hide the sketch layer
shown in Figure 3.7, because it is in the **Default** or **Normal Composite
Method**, which is completely opaque. Choose **Multiply** from the pop-up
list. Figure 3.8 shows that method works nicely to combine both layers.
Continue painting on your color layer, but keep it loose.

Figure 3.8 Blended layers.

Source: Corel ® Corporation.
Art © 2014 Cengage Learning.

Figure 3.7 Opaque paint.

© 2014 Cengage Learning.

Do Play with Your Food

My judgment about the painting at this stage, shown in Figure 3.9, is that the pencil sketch is overpowering the color layer. There are ways to fix that. You can try lowering the opacity of the sketch, but opacity controls are not available for the "background" canvas. You'll have to turn the canvas into a layer first. It's easy: **Select All (Cmd/Ctrl+A)**, **Cut (Cmd/Ctrl+X)**, and **Paste (Cmd/Ctrl+V)**. Now that the sketch is on top of the color layer, choose **Multiply** once again to reveal the layer below.

Turn the opacity of this sketch layer down as needed. Figure 3.10 shows the **Layers** panel with sketch opacity at 40%. I like the result, shown in Figure 3.11, but there should be stronger darks here and there, as well as some lighter highlights to accent the onions and other bits.

Figure 3.10 Sketch over, color under.

Source: Corel ® Corporation.
Art © 2014 Cengage Learning.

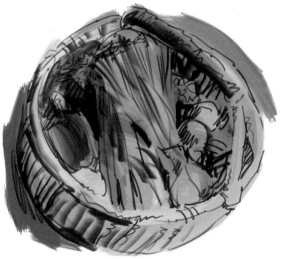

Figure 3.9 Pencil power.

© 2014 Cengage Learning.

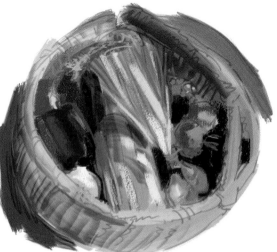

Figure 3.11 Bland veggies.

© 2014 Cengage Learning.

Labels for Layers

Layers will automatically have numbers, whch can be changed to descriptive names, just as you would change the name of a file or folder. Just tap on the **Layer 2** name, for example, and it becomes an editable field for typing in the new name.

Make a new layer and allow it to remain in the **Default Composite Method**. Choose the old familiar **Square Hard Pastel** or another variant from the **Pastels** category. Use **Real Soft Conte** (in your custom palette) for thinner lines and details. Sample colors either in the **Reference Image** or by using the **Dropper** tool directly on your working image. Just use the **Option/Alt** key to get the **Dropper** function to click on the color you want. Then let go of the modifier key, and you're ready to paint again.

Figure 3.12 shows my finished piece. You'll want to save your work as a Painter RIFF file to keep the layers separate (or PSD if you plan to alter it in Photoshop). When you are ready, flatten the image by using the **Drop All** command in the **Layers** menu, and then click **Save As** in a more convenient and compressed format, such as JPEG.

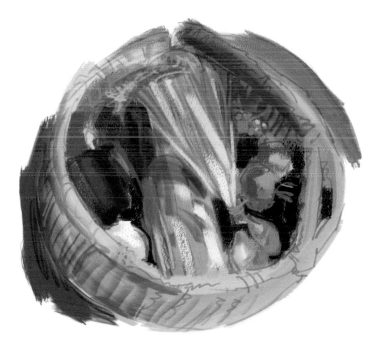

Figure 3.12 Fresh and crispy.

Extra Cheese

After all the fruit and vegetables, it's time I offered something to the carnivores. Open **personal_pepperoni.jpg**, shown in Figure 3.13. There is a border of white at the top. Add about 50 pixels to the bottom and each side, so you'll have some room for brush strokes to go beyond the edges of the photo.

You'll create two versions of this photo: deep dish and thin crust. *Just kidding!* One will be a fine art oil painting and the other an illustration suitable for an ad campaign. Start with the oil painting.

Figure 3.13 Hot and spicy.

Paint Your Lunch

Use **File > Clone** (not Quick Clone) to make a copy of the photo that automatically establishes the original as a clone source. You'll make changes to the copy and use the original image as a safety net. You can undo any changes that you don't like by using a **Cloner** brush to retrieve the original pixels wherever you want them.

Cut to the Quick

It could actually be quicker to work with a **Clone** instead of a **Quick Clone**! With the **Quick Clone** option, you're working on a blank canvas and must re-create everything. With a **Clone** copy, you'll have more choices: change only portions of the image, for example, or apply an effect to the entire image and use a **Cloner** brush to retrieve some areas from the original state.

Your oil painting of the pizza will rely on two brushes: **Coarse Oily Blender** and **Camel Oil Cloner**. Make a small custom palette with those two items, so you can switch between them easily. Use **Coarse Oily Blender** to smear the pizza photo until it looks something like the messy version shown in Figure 3.14. Be sure to maintain the essence of the image by using short, curved strokes that follow the contours of the plate and vertical strokes for the two shakers. Smear past the hard edge into the white border to make an irregular edge. The image should be just barely recognizable.

Bring some of the orignal detail back, gently, using the **Camel Oil Cloner**. Let the background and most of the plate remain smeary, but tease out a few areas that need to be redefined. In my work, the shakers required some shiny bits and a little more to the shape of the glass containers. Some of the pepperoni slices could use a bit more crispiness. Figure 3.15 is well done.

Figure 3.14 Extra gooey.
© 2014 Cengage Learning.

Figure 3.15 Pass me a napkin.
© 2014 Cengage Learning.

If this were a traditional oil painting on canvas, some of the canvas texture would show through. You can create that, using **Effects > Surface Control > Apply Surface Texture**. When the dialog box comes up, as shown in Figure 3.16, be sure to have **Paper** in the **Using** field. It will show how the currently selected paper will look, and you can switch textures without closing the dialog. Choose **Coarse Cotton Canvas** from the **Paper** library. The only setting you'll need to change is **Appearance of Depth: Amount**. Use the Preview window to help you decide how much texture to apply. If the effect is too strong, use the **Edit > Fade** command to reduce the effect by any percentage you want. My finished painting is shown in Figure 3.17.

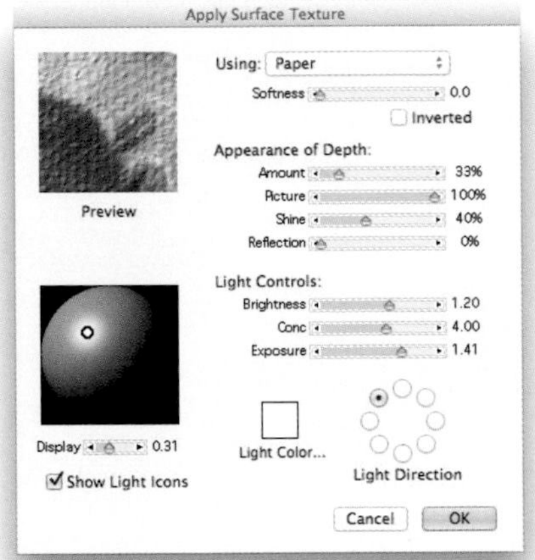

fade In

The **Fade** command in the **Edit** menu is a powerful tool for reducing the strength of your last effect. It can also be used to partially undo your previous brush stroke.

Figure 3.16 Extra texture.

Source: Corel ® Corporation.

Figure 3.17 Good enough to eat or hang.

Special f/x Sauce

Open the original pepperoni pizza photo again, so you can make another version. Create a second layer that is the same as the canvas. No need to use the **New Layer** command. Just **Select All**, and **Copy (Cmd/Ctrl+C)**, and then **Paste**. Pasting automatically creates a new layer, and the original image on the canvas is untouched. You'll apply a few special effects to the new layer and explore various composite methods for blending them with the original canvas image.

Choose **Effects > Surface Control > Distress**, using the settings shown in Figure 3.18. *Grain* is another term for paper texture. To get a fine grain, use **Hot Press Paper**. The results are shown in Figure 3.19. The original image underneath is completely hidden. Can you recall how to make all those white pixels transparent? Figure 3.20 shows the composite image with the distressed layer using the **Gel** or **Multiply** method. The result has the look of an antique or vintage poster. It's perfect for an ad campaign about the old-time goodness of industrially processed food-like substances.

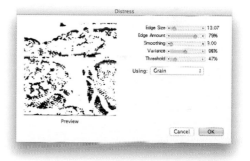

Figure 3.18 Distress multiplied.

Source: Corel ® Corporation.

Figure 3.19 Distressing settings.

© 2014 Cengage Learning.

Figure 3.20 Extra grainy.

© 2014 Cengage Learning.

The **Surface Control** category in the **Effects** menu includes some other choices that are similar to the **Distress** effect. Try using **Express Texture**, **Sketch**, or **Woodcut**. The **Woodcut** effect has several controls for manipulating the black edges and colors independently. Figure 3.21 shows settings that produced the results shown in Figure 3.22.

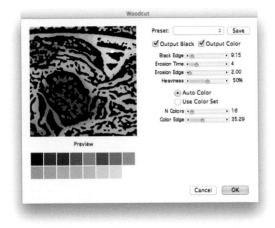

The "secret sauce" in this very bold graphic is the **Hard Light Composite Method**. If you want to reduce the effect somewhat, simply lower the opacity of the layer with the slider in the **Layers** panel. This is safer than using the **Edit > Fade** command, because you can increase opacity again later.

Figure 3.21 Wood grain.

Source: Corel ® Corporation. Art © 2014 Cengage Learning.

Figure 3.22 Hard cheese.

© 2014 Cengage Learning.

Suppose you want to reduce or eliminate the **Woodcut** effect in only some areas of the layer, but not the whole layer. You could use the eraser tool, but there is a better way that will allow you to change your mind at any time, until you flatten the image. Make a layer mask, as shown in Figure 3.23. Refer to Figure 3.5 if you need to find the appropriate icon at the bottom of the **Layers** panel.

The **Woodcut** effect has made the crushed red pepper in the shaker too black. You can reveal the original pixels from the underlying canvas image by painting on the layer mask with black. Yes, that sounds counterintuitive until you read the note "Unmasking a Technique."

Figure 3.23 White mask.

Source: Corel ® Corporation.
Art © 2014 Cengage Learning.

Unmasking a Technique

Don't be afraid of the "M" word. The basic rule is simply this: **white reveals and black conceals**. A fresh new layer mask is completely white, indicating that all pixels on the layer are fully revealed. To hide any part of the layer, paint on its layer mask with black. Shades of gray partially conceal pixels. Painting with white completely reveals the pixels once again.

I used an Oil Pastel with black to make the change shown in Figure 3.24. Figure 3.25 shows a tiny black area on the layer mask that corresponds to the part of the pepper shaker that has the woodcut effect removed. If you want to retrieve the woodcut effect in that area later, simply paint on the layer mask with white.

Figure 3.24 Crushed pepper, before and after.

© 2014 Cengage Learning.

Figure 3.25 Layer mask with black.

Source: Corel ® Corporation.
Art © 2014 Cengage Learning.

When you're satisfied with the composite, use the **Drop** command in the **Layers** menu to commit to your changes and flatten the image. Use **Save As** to give your image a new name, choosing any file format you prefer. It's a good idea to save the layered image in Painter's native Riff file format also.

Layered Cake

Do you still have room for dessert? Good. Make a new image about 1600 pixels wide and 900 pixels high. Choose a light blue for the paper color. Open **cupcake_rack.jpg**, shown in Figure 3.26. Use the **Lasso** tool to select one of the cupcakes. Copy it (**Cmd/Ctrl+C**) and paste it (**Cmd/Ctrl+V**) on the new blank canvas. The cupcake now occupies its own layer. Clean up the edges of the cupcake with an eraser variant, such as **Real Pointy Eraser**. Make another identical cupcake layer by holding the **Option/Alt** key while you drag the cupcake to another position, using the **Layer Adjuster** tool. There are now two of them, each on its own layer. Repeat the same sequence of steps for two or three different cupcakes.

Figure 3.26 Let us eat cake.

© 2014 Cengage Learning.

Your new image should look something like what is shown in Figure 3.27.

Figure 3.27 Eight cupcakes.

© 2014 Cengage Learning.

Supersize Me

The cupcakes need to be bigger. (I've said that so often!) You'll take advantage of a new feature in Painter X3: transform across layers. No need to enlarge each cupcake separately. Just select all layers by targeting the top one and **Shift**-clicking the bottom one, as shown in Figure 3.28.

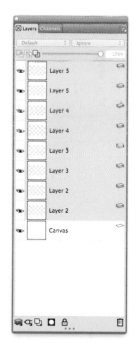

Figure 3.28 Eight-layer cake.

Source: Corel ® Corporation

53

When you choose the **Transform** tool, which shares a space with the **Layer Adjuster** tool, your cupcakes will temporarily look like grayish blobs, as shown in Figure 3.29. Hold down the **Shift** key and drag a corner handle of the bounding box out until the cupcakes are the size you want. The **Shift** key will constrain the proportions of the cupcakes.

Arrange the cupcakes in a grid, similar to the one in Figure 3.30.

Make a **Quick Clone** of the cupcake grid and check the **Show Source Image** box in the **Clone Source** panel.

Figure 3.29 Let them eat blobs!

© 2014 Cengage Learning.

Target Your Pixels

You might want to have the **Clone Source** image open while you work on a clone painting. The crosshair cursor comes in handy if you want to use the source image as reference without relying completely on **Tracing Paper**.

Figure 3.30 Grid cakes.

© 2014 Cengage Learning.

Now you're ready to reinterpret the cupcakes in a variety of styles. Although there are many **Cloner** brushes to choose from, you can turn any variant into a **Cloner** by using the **Clone Color** option on the color picker. It's the Rubber Stamp icon.

Clone Me

Experiment with several **Cloner** variants and "regular" variants with **Clone Color** enabled, to create a sampler of cupcakes. My version is shown in Figure 3.31.

Figure 3.31 Cloned cakes.

© 2014 Cengage Learning.

I used brushes in the custom palette shown in Figure 3.32. The positon of each brush icon in the custom palette matches the positon of its cupcake in the grid. Five of the brushes are **Cloner** variants, so they all share the same **Rubber Stamp** icon. To help identify them, place your cursor over any icon and right-click (**Ctrl**-click on the Mac); then choose the **View as Text** option in the pop-up list.

The remaining four brushes are **Dry Ink** (Pens category), **Sargent Brush** (Artists category, named for the famous nineteenth century portrait painter, John Singer Sargent), **Gloopy** (Impasto), and **Gouache Rake Jitter** (Gouache). To use those variants as cloners, you must enable **Clone Color** in the color picker. There are nine brushes to eight cupcakes because I used two of them on the last image, lower right: **Gloopy** for the frosting and **Gouache Rake Jitter** for the muffin cup.

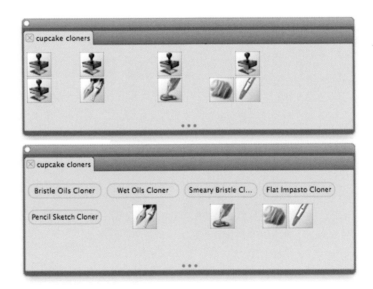

Figure 3.32 Spelled out.

Source: Corel ® Corporation.

What's Next?

Congratulations! You've covered most of the essential food groups, including two of the three "Cs"—cheese and chocolate. The third one, of course, is caffeine.

You've had considerable exposure to layers and cloning. You got a taste of composite methods—enough to see how powerful they can be in the development of artwork. In upcoming lessons, you'll work with a variety of subject matters, styles, and techniques. Brush controls will be introduced, so you can understand the anatomy of a Painter brush and how to bend it to your will. But first, grab some coffee and a snack. You earned it.

4 The Great Outdoors

In this lesson, you'll paint some outdoor scenes, but you won't have to worry about carrying sunscreen or rain gear. Later on, you can pack a lunch with your laptop and set out for digital *plein aire* painting in the park. But for now, enjoy the comfort and safety of home, protected from the criticism of nosy neighbors or rude tourists.

For this lesson you'll use

• **Images:** depot_cafe.jpg, sunset1.jpg

Coffee Break

Open **depot_cafe.jpg**, shown in Figure 4.1, as a Reference Image. Zoom in as needed, and stretch the window to view the entire image. It's a relatively simple scene, and you'll simplify it even more when you create a pastel painting of the scene. Make a custom palette containing **Square Grainy Pastel**, **Flat Grainy Stump** (a Blender), and **Real Soft Conte**.

Use **File > New (Cmd/Ctrl+N)** to make a new canvas 1066 pixels (px) wide × 1149 px high. Accept the default paper color and texture, for now. Many pastel artists use tinted paper, and you will do the same. The muted pink in the arched strip over the awnings is an ideal paper color for this project. Sample it with the **Dropper** tool and use **Canvas > Set Paper Color**. To fill the white canvas with the new color, use **Select > All** and **Delete/Backspace**. Your blank canvas should now be pink.

Here's What Happened

Painter defines **Paper Color** as whatever an eraser reveals. When you select a new current color, choose **Set Paper Color** followed by the select-and-delete maneuver, you have basically erased the entire canvas, revealing the new color.

Pastel Painting

Use **Square Grainy Pastel** to boldly "rough in" the major shapes. Sample colors in the Reference Image with the **Dropper** tool. Ignore the woman sitting at the table and all the vaguely visible furniture behind the railing. Figure 4.2 shows the basic shapes and colors sketched in. Allow the paper to show in the places where there is pink in the image.

Figure 4.1 Cafe scene.

© 2014 Cengage Learning.

Figure 4.2 Roughing it.

© 2014 Cengage Learning.

Add some detail with **Real Soft Conte** and smooth out some rough areas with the **Flat Grainy Stump** blender. The tile roof is more of a challenge. Use a combination of angled vertical strokes and short horizontal curves, with three or four sampled colors. Figure 4.3 shows my work at this stage.

Figure 4.3 Smoothing it.

© 2014 Cengage Learning.

Basic Paper texture works fine for most of the drawing, but some areas—the greenery in the foreground and the roof tiles—could benefit from bolder surface effects. Open both **Paper** panels from the **Window** menu and choose **Sandy Pastel Paper**, as shown in Figure 4.4.

Figure 4.4 Switch your swatch.

Source: Corel ® Corporation.

Paper Work

Sandy Pastel Paper has an organic variation to the grain, but it's much too fine for this painting. Increase the size of the grain to about 300%, as shown in Figure 4.5. Develop the foliage with your pastel and conte sticks, using lighter green for the upper areas. Your work should look something like the detail in Figure 4.6.

Figure 4.5 Sandy on steroids.

Source. Corel ® Corporation.

Figure 4.6 From sandy to leafy.

© 2014 Cengage Learning.

Rather than search through Painter's alternate paper libraries for a roof tile texture, if there is one, you'll save time by making one from the original photo. Drag the **Rectangular Selection** tool over several tiles in the roof, as shown in Figure 4.7.

Figure 4.7 Tiles for a tile.

© 2014 Cengage Learning.

Use the **Capture Paper** command in the **Papers** pop-up menu, shown in Figure 4.8. Save your new paper tile as **Roof tiles**, using a cross-fade setting of about 40. Cross-fade helps to soften the edges of a tile, useful to create the illusion of a seamless texture.

Paper Trail

A texture in Painter is simply a rectangular grayscale image element that repeats as a seamless tile. It carries no color information. You choose color whenever you use the selected paper with brush variants whose behavior is designed to express paper grain.

Figure 4.8 Grab it.

Your custom paper is now the last item in your current paper library. The size is perfect, of course, but you might want to increase contrast and brightness to get a stronger grain effect. Figure 4.9 shows your new paper before and after those adjustments.

Figure 4.9 Tile style.

Now that you have the ideal paper texture for the roof, apply some pastel strokes with color variations sampled from the photo. Invert the paper, as shown in Figure 4.10, for lighter colors on the upper curves. Figure 4.11 shows the finished effect.

Figure 4.10 Negative tile.

Source: Corel ® Corporation.
Art © 2014 Cengage Learning.

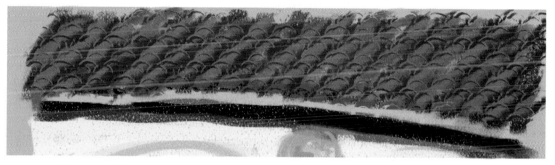

Figure 4.11 Roof and ready.

© 2014 Cengage Learning.

Let Us Spray

The next project is an airbrush graphic. Real-world airbrushes spray tiny droplets of pigment mixed with compressed air. The instrument connected to that compressed air source is a device with a nozzle and a small reservoir for pigment. It has a couple of tiny wheels for finger control of the size of the spray and the density and coarseness of the droplets. It takes quite a bit of practice to acquire skill with this tool. Painter lets you shave months, even years, off that process.

In traditional airbrush painting, portions of the paper or other surface are protected from paint or ink with a mask. These can be made from tape or cardboard or self-adhesive frisket paper cut to the precise shape needed. It shouldn't surprise you that for digital airbrush art, creating masks is much easier.

Pixel-based applications like Painter (and Photoshop) provide several tools for selecting portions of the canvas to accept painted strokes or effects. Whatever isn't selected is, by definition, masked. You can make perfect rectangular and oval selections using one of the tools sharing a space in the **Toolbox**, or you can draw freehand selections around an irregular area using the **Lasso** tool. The **Polygon Lasso** tool is handy for selecting any shape with straight edges. A sophisticated selection tool that has no counterpart in traditional media is the **Magic Wand**, which selects all pixels in a defined color range. Refer back to Figure 1.5 in Lesson 1, "The Basics," to see where the selection tools are located. Notice the **Selection Adjuster** tool, which allows you to move or alter a selection marquee. Choices are available in the **Property Bar** for adding to or subtracting from a selection using any of the selection tools. This allows you to create some complex selection areas.

When the Ants Come Marching In

An active selection is surrounded by a marquee that looks like an animated dashed line. The cute nickname for this is *marching ants*. You might want to turn off the marching ants (without losing the selection) to see your work better. The **Hide/Show Marquee** toggle in the **Select** menu has a keyboard shortcut: **Shift Cmd/Ctrl+H**.

You can apply paint to a selection without having to be careful at the edges. You can also use the **Paint Bucket** tool to fill a selection instantly with your choice from the **Property Bar**: current color, gradient, pattern, or weave. An especially dandy command in the **Select** menu is **Stroke Selection**. This will automatically paint the edges of your selection, using the current brush variant.

Air Quality

Make a new canvas, any size, for trying out several of the **Airbrush** variants. Figure 4.12 shows a custom palette with four Airbrush variants, and strokes made with each of them are shown in Figure 4.13. Remember the trick you learned in Lesson 3, "Take a Layer," for changing the category icon into the name of the variant? To remind you, place your cursor over any icon and right-click (**Ctrl**-click on the Mac); then choose the **View as Text** option in the pop-up list.

Figure 4.12 Coarse Spray Jitter and friends.

Source: Corel ® Corporation.

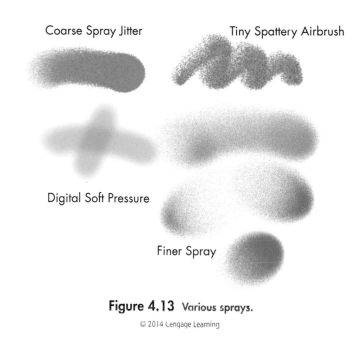

Coarse Spray Jitter

Tiny Spattery Airbrush

Digital Soft Pressure

Finer Spray

Figure 4.13 Various sprays.

© 2014 Cengage Learning

Many of the **Airbrush** variants, such as **Finer Spray**, respond to the tilt of your Wacom stylus, creating a realistic directional spray of pigment. Notice that the **Digital Soft Pressure Airbrush** has a fine spray that applies pigment at a low opacity, so you can spray over the same area to build up color. **Coarse Spray Jitter** has a small amount of variability in the saturation and value of the sprayed droplets. **Tiny Spattery Airbrush** is noticeably coarser and has greater color variability. Variation in hue (H), saturation (S), or value (V) can be determined with sliders in the **Color Variability** panel, shown in Figure 4.14. You can choose other parameters for creating color variability with options in the pop-up list: using RGB instead of HSV, or colors from the current Gradient or Color Set.

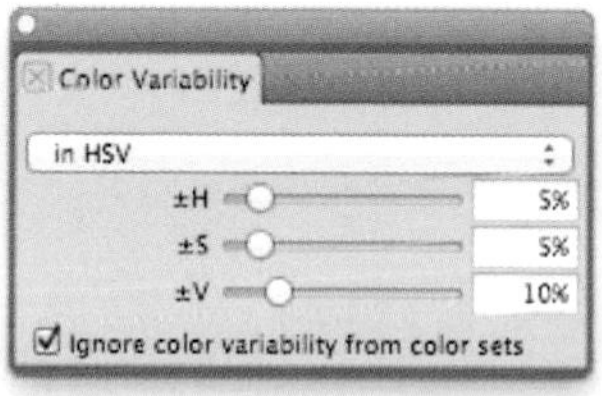

Figure 4.14 Try the Gradient option.

Source: Corel ® Corporation.

Figure 4.15 shows changes in color variability made to the default **Tiny Spattery Airbrush** (top stroke). The middle stroke has H, S, and V variabaility turned up to about 30% each. The bottom stroke uses the **Vivid Colored Stripes** gradient to determine color variations.

Figure 4.15 Variation versatility.

© 2014 Cengage Learning.

Air Apparent

Painter provides a portfolio of ready-made selections, shown in Figure 4.16. Find them using **Window > Media Library Panels > Selections**. To use one, double-click its icon, and the "marching ants" will appear on your canvas. Move or transform this "marquee" with the **Selection Adjuster** tool.

Figure 4.16 The selection collection.

Source: Corel ® Corporation.

Major Adjustments

Use the **Selection Adjuster** not only to move a selection, but to resize, distort, and rotate it. When you choose the **Selection Adjuster** tool and click on an active selection, eight tiny black handles will appear, as shown in Figure 4.17. Drag the appropriate handle to scale the selection, with the **Shift** key held to maintain its proportions. To tilt a selection, press the **Cmd/Ctrl** key and hover your stylus over a corner handle until the cursor becomes a rotate symbol. Then drag the handle to any angle you desire. Warning: don't confuse the **Selection Adjuster** with the **Layer Adjuster**!

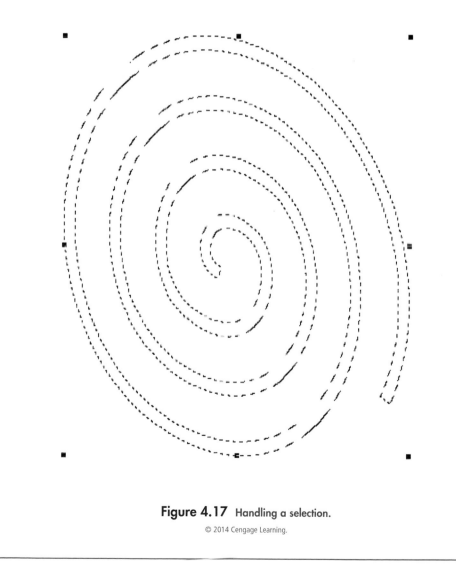

Figure 4.17 Handling a selection.

© 2014 Cengage Learning.

Create airbrush samples similar to those shown in Figure 4.18. The hearts, spirals, and sphere were made with items from the selection portfolio. The fluffy cloud began with a freehand **Lasso** selection.

- A spiral selection was distorted with the **Selection Adjuster** and painted with **Finer Spray**. Then the selection was moved a few pixels up and to the left and sprayed with **Tiny Spattery Airbrush**. I switched to the **Scratchboard** tool and chose black for applying the **Stroke Selection** command.

- A green sphere was made with **Finer Spray**, concentrating pigment on the left. A small highlight on the right helps to create the illusion of volume. With a little practice, you can create smooth gradients "by hand."

- The first three hearts were made with **Finer Spray**, allowing the pigment to trail off, creating some transparency. The fourth heart uses the **Stroke Selection** command with a **Pattern Pen**. The pattern I chose, **Lotus Petals**, is explored in Figure 4.19.

- Our fluffy cloud was filled with two colors. Then, using the **Invert Selection** command to protect the cloud, I sprayed color "behind" it. That is a good way to make a drop shadow effect also.

Figure 4.18 Airbrush practice.

© 2014 Cengage Learning.

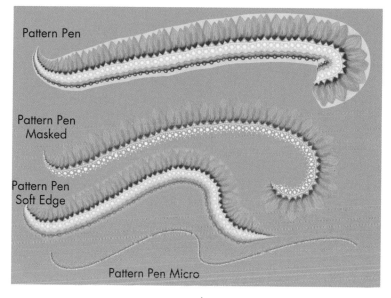

Figure 4.19 Pattern Pen variants.

© 2014 Cengage Learning.

Hawaiian Sunset

Open **sunset1.jpg** from my collection of photos taken on the island of Kauai.
It will be hard to improve on nature, shown in Figure 4.20, but let's give it a try.
You'll make a postcard graphic using selection techniques and airbrush painting.

Figure 4.20 Natural beauty.

© 2014 Cengage Learning.

Use the **Magic Wand** tool to select the palm tree. With the tolerance raised to about 45, you should pick up most of those black and almost black pixels. If you need to add to your selection, enable the corresponding icon in the **Property Bar**, shown in Figure 4.21, or hold down the **Shift** key and click in the area you want to add. Some of the darkest water pixels might have been picked up. To remove them from the selection, use (you guessed it!) the **Subtract from Selection** icon, or hold the **Opt/Alt** key and use the **Rectanglar** or **Lasso** selection tool to clean things up. Don't worry about not picking up the delicate tips of the palm fronds. Your marching ants should look similar to those in Figure 4.22. Save the tree selection, using the command at the botton of the **Selection** menu. You will be using it again soon. Figure 4.23 shows the Save Selection dialog, where you can give your selection a distinctive name.

Tolerate This!

The **Magic Wand** selects pixels that are similar in color or value. Tolerance is a variable that determines how much similarity in color is required for inclusion in a selection. Lower the tolerance to restrict the selection to fewer degrees of similartiy. Raise the tolerance to expand the range of colors or values that are selected. Another tool with a tolerance setting is the **Paint Bucket**.

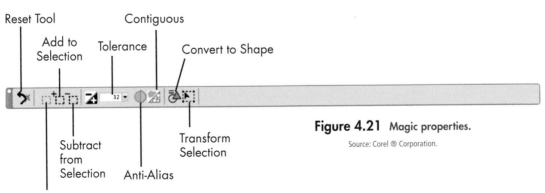

Figure 4.21 Magic properties.

Source: Corel ® Corporation.

Figure 4.22 Select a tree.

© 2014 Cengage Learning.

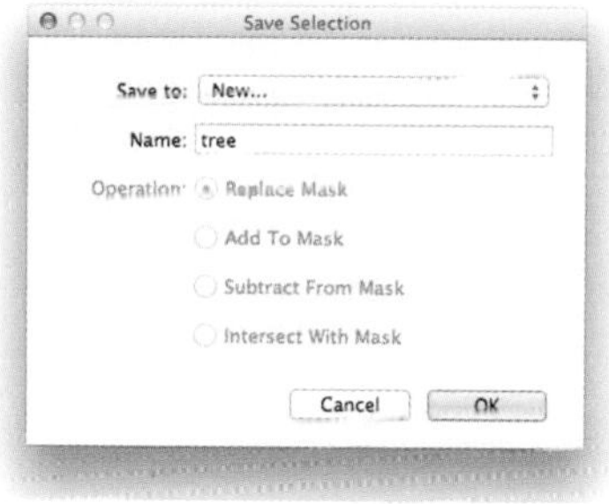

Figure 4.23 Save a tree.

Source: Corel ® Corporation.

Get Saved

Make five or six more selections of areas that are similar in color, and save each selection to a new channel. For example, select the three major cloud shapes and save them as a single selection. Figure 4.24 shows the descriptive names of all the selections I saved for this image.

How Touching!

When the **Contiguous** option in the **Property Bar** for the **Magic Wand** is engaged (blue), only similar pixels that are touching each other will be selected. Same-color pixels that are separated from the group will not be selected. If you want to include all the similar pixels in the entire image, turn off this feature.

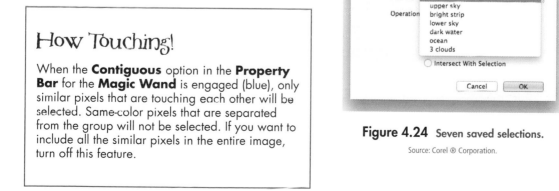

Figure 4.24 Seven saved selections.

Source: Corel ® Corporation.

To select all the pale blue pixels in the upper part of the sky, I turned the **Contiguous** option off, so all the similar pixels mixed in with the tree shape on the right would be included.

When you have all your selections saved, delete the image and fill the blank with any background color you want. I'm using a golden yellow.

Get Loaded

Load each of the saved selections one at a time and use a variety of **Airbrush** variants or **Paint Bucket** fills to color them.

Channeling

Open the **Channels** panel, shown in Figure 4.25. It shows each of the selections you saved. Turn off visibility of the RGB image and make the tree channel visible, as shown in Figure 4.26. It is solid white against black. Recall that in a layer mask, white reveals and black conceals. This white image is basicaly a mask that can be loaded as a selection. You can make very detailed selections by painting with black, white, or shades of gray directly on a channel.

Figure 4.25 Channels, selections, and masks, oh my!

Source: Corel ® Corporation. Art © 2014 Cengage Learning.

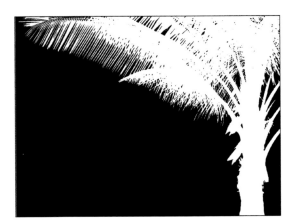

Figure 4.26 The tree channel.

© 2014 Cengage Learning.

I loaded the tree channel and used a **Paint Bucket** fill with the two-point gradient preset. My primary color is a saturated purple and the secondary color a slightly muted shade. The effect is a subtle gradation from rich color in the trunk that fades into the fronds. Next, I loaded the water channel and switched to the **Tiny Spattery Airbrush**. Streaks of lighter shades were made using long horizontal stokes. This stage is shown in Figure 4.27.

Figure 4.27 Purple and blue.

© 2014 Cengage Learning.

The upper sky was filled with the **Paint Bucket** using a solid light yellow. The center strip was painted with the **Digital Soft Pressure Airbrush** in a couple of different orange colors. I wasn't really happy with the selection for "dark water," so I altered it by painting with black and white in the channel and using a smeary blender to create shades of gray. These would become areas of partial selection. Take a few minutes to repair any of your channels that could use improvement. My new channel is shown in Figure 4.28, and the effect of a dark blue fill is shown in Figure 4.29.

Figure 4.28 Change the channel.

© 2014 Cengage Learning.

Figure 4.29 Deep blue sea.

© 2014 Cengage Learning.

To give the cloud shapes some pizzazz, I used a technique similar to the practice cloud in Figure 4.18. Spray the whole cloud with pale yellow, and then use **Finer Spray** to gently darken the bottom with variable orange droplets. Finally, invert the selection to spray a darker color around the bottom of the cloud. I switched to the **Digital Soft Pressure** variant for that last step. Figure 4.30 shows my finished postcard. Is it really finished? As long as you have all those channels, you can make any number of variations.

Figure 4.30 Aloha!

© 2014 Cengage Learning.

What's Next?

You can be proud of yourself for completing some challenging projects. Working with masks and channels is considered, by some, to be difficult. But we showed them, didn't we? With that kind of confidence, you'll have no trouble drawing and painting human subjects. Portraits await you in the next lesson.

5 Painting People

Capturing the likeness of your granny is a much bigger challenge than making an apple look like a Granny Smith. Tracing and cloning a photo will handle the essential matters of accuracy and proportion. Beyond that is a vast array of choices for interpreting your subject. You'll get some practice doing just that in the following projects.

For this lesson you'll use

- **Images:** hines_guitar2.jpg, ken_arms-crossed.jpg, emily_profile.jpg

Watercolor Portrait

Open the photo of Hines and his guitar, shown in Figure 5.1. This image already has a good composition and an interesting arrangement of tones and shapes with a minimal color range. Choose the Watercolor scheme from the **Color Scheme** list in the **Underpainting** panel, one of the **Auto-Painting** panels, shown in Figure 5.2.

Figure 5.1 The Artist Hines. (That's his legal name!)

© 2014 Cengage Learning.

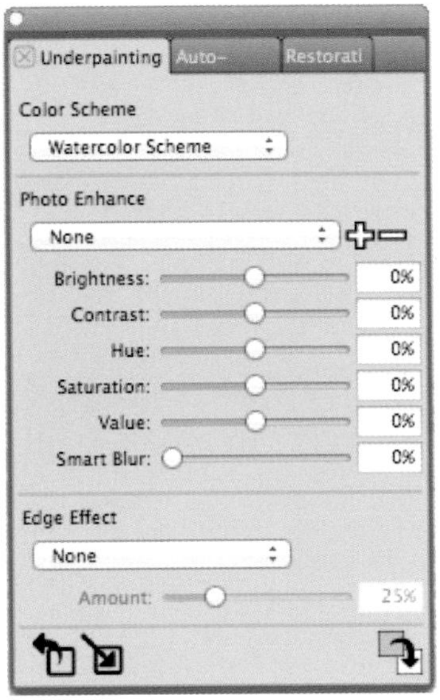

Figure 5.2 Change of color.

Source: Corel ® Corporation.

The effect is a much lighter and brighter image, shown in Figure 5.3, revealing more detail in the folds of the jacket. Make a **Quick Clone** of this version and use **Tracing Paper** to sketch the basic outlines of the figure and the guitar. Use **Sketching Pencil 5** and a dark brown color to complete a rough sketch, similar to the one shown in Figure 5.4.

Figure 5.3 Lighter and brighter.

© 2014 Cengage Learning.

Figure 5.4 Quick sketch.

© 2014 Cengage Learning.

Introduction to Watercolor

Load the lightened version of the photo as your Reference Image. You will add water-color to your sketch of Hines, sampling color from the Reference Image. But first, get aquainted with several of the **Digital Watercolor** variants, especially those shown in Figure 5.5. The strokes were all made with the same shade of blue. Make a custom palette for these variants, as shown in Figure 5.6. You can add more variants as you work or delete the ones that don't work for you.

Water, Water Everywhere!

Painter X3 provides two separate categories for Watercolor brushes. **Digital Watercolor** variants are relatively simple and intuitive. The more advanced **Watercolor** brushes require a special layer and may take more practice to master, possibly even more than is required with traditional watercolor techniques.

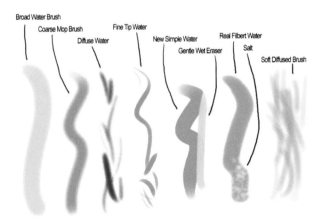

Figure 5.5 Digital watercolor strokes.

© 2014 Cengage Learning.

Figure 5.6 Digital watercolor palette.

Source: Corel ® Corporation.

82

Make a new layer for the watercolor stage, so you can keep it separate from your rough sketch. An ordinary or default layer is fine, because this category does not require the special **Watercolor** layer. Work from light to dark, gradually building up color. Begin with larger brush sizes such as the **Broad Water Brush** or **Real Filbert Watercolor**. Details can be made with **Fine Tip Water** as finishing touches. Figure 5.7 shows the first application of water color strokes. Hines' jacket is black, but the watercolor scheme gave it a muted green tint. It's wise to avoid black when emulating watercolor. Your painting is much more lively when color is built up to create rich shadows and tones that combine colors other than black.

Figure 5.7 Add color.

© 2014 Cengage Learning.

Always Room for Gel Mode

When you made your first stroke with a **Watercolor** variant on the new layer, Painter automatically switched from the default (opaque) composite method to Gel. This makes sense, because the essence of watercolor is transparency.

Big Buildup

In developing Hines's face, I added another layer so I could control the buildup of pigment. This technique is similar to allowing one layer of traditional watercolor to dry before adding additional paint. Figure 5.8 shows the two color layers separately, along with the composite.

Figure 5.8 Wet over dry.

The finished piece, shown in Figure 5.9, includes some background color applied with the **Broad Water Brush** and enhanced with a few sprinkles of **Salt**. Traditional watercolorists use coarse salt to produce a similar sparkly effect. The salt crystals absorb wet pigment, revealing the white paper. After the piece dries, you simply brush away the salt. Incidentally, if you want to retain the wetness of Watercolor layers, to work on them later, simply save your painting in RIFF format.

Figure 5.9 Completely dry.

Oil and Acrylic Portrait

Open the photo of Ken with his arms crossed, shown in Figure 5.10. You'll capture Ken's pose in digital oils and have some fun making an abstract background based on the colorful artwork behind him.

Figure 5.10 Photo of Ken.

© 2014 Cengage Learning.

Figure Versus Ground

First, fill the blank spaces around Ken's head with colors derived from the two paintings. One way to do that is with the **Cloner** tool. (Refer to Figure 1.5 in Lesson 1, "Let's Get Started," if you're not sure where to find it.) You'll use a method called offset cloning or point-to-point cloning. Hold down the **Option/Alt** key and tap your stylus near the top of the right-hand painting. A little green dot with the number "1" appears, indicating that you have established a source pixel. Release the modifier key. Choose the **Straight Cloner** from the **Cloner** brush variants and begin painting at the top edge of the photo, as shown in Figure 5.11. Repeat the method for the left side of the photo. You can establish a different source pixel whenever you want to. Fill up the spaces completely, as shown in Figure 5.12.

Figure 5.11 Fill in the blanks.

© 2014 Cengage Learning.

Figure 5.12 All full.

Overdone?

Did you get so enthusiasic with your cloning that you accidentally covered up one of Ken's ears or the top of his bald head? No worries. Just use the **Clone Source** panel to establish the original photo as your source. Then use the **Straight Cloner** to bring back any Ken pixels you lost.

You will treat the figure of Ken differently from the background. As you work, you'll want to protect Ken's head and body from intrusion by your background painting. Make a lasso selection of the figure and save the selection. (See Lesson 4, "The Great Outdoors," for details on saving and loading selections.) Figure 5.13 shows the new channel created when you saved the selection.

Figure 5.13 Ken-shaped channel.

Invert the selection **(Cmd/Ctrl+I)** so that only the background will accept paint or effects. Find the **Smeary Varnish** variant in the **Impasto** category and use it to create the look of thick brush strokes as you smear away details in the background. Your results should look similar to Figure 5.14. Begin a new custom palette with this brush, by **Shift**-dragging its icon to your workspace. You'll be using other **Impasto** variants, which all have the same category icon. Use the right-click method (**Ctrl**-click on the Mac) to view the name of the brush variant instead of the category icon.

Figure 5.14 Background brushwork.

© 2014 Cengage Learning.

Oil Versus Water

Your goal is to make the background appear to be painted in acrylics and then apply an oil painting style to the figure.

Mixing Media

Acrylic paints are water based. In traditional media, you would never mix them with an oil-based medium. One exception is that you may paint with oils over acrylic paint that has thoroughly dried. Painter X3, however, allows you to mix oil and water without fear!

Create the look of extra heavy gels or fiber paste, which acrylic painters apply to canvas or panels to develop sculptured surfaces. Be sure that the figure is still masked, and use **Effects > Surface Control > Apply Surface Texture**. Figure 5.15 shows the settings I used. It's very important to choose Image Luminance in the **Using** field. Softness and Amount are also important variables. If the effect is too strong, use **Edit > Fade** to reduce it. My results are shown in Figure 5.16.

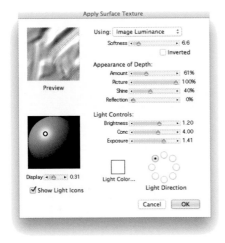

Figure 5.15 Soft depth.

Source: Corel ® Corporation.

Figure 5.16 Deep background.

© 2014 Cengage Learning.

You can increase the vibrancy of the background by using **Tonal Control > Adjust Colors**. Increase Saturation to about 25%, as shown in Figure 5.17.

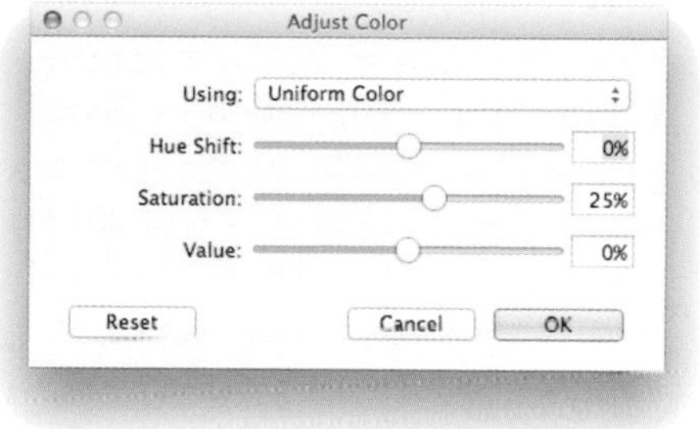

Figure 5.17 Punch up the color.

Source: Corel ® Corporation.

Invert the selection, so you can work on Ken. Use **Camel Impasto Cloner** to make brush strokes following the contours of his face and arms, as well as the shirt. Add this variant to your custom palette. Figure 5.18 shows a detail of my work at this stage.

Figure 5.18 Up close and Impasto.

© 2014 Cengage Learning.

Invert the selection once again so you can add more stuff to the background. Use the **Gloopy** variant of the **Impasto** category to make thick swirls and squiggles and some 3D droplets. Try a few strokes with the **Depth Rake**, another **Impasto** brush. The **Depth Smear** variant allows you to soften some areas. Have fun with it! If your background gets so busy that it takes attention away from Ken, consider a lighting effect. **Effects > Surface Control > Apply Lighting** brings up the dialog shown in Figure 5.19. Be sure to deselect (**Cmd/Ctrl+D**) so that the lighting will affect the entire image. I chose the **Warm Globe** preset to bring focus to the figure, as shown in Figure 5.20.

Let There Be Lights

You can add multiple lights to your image by clicking on the **Apply Lighting** image preview dialog box. Each light is controlled by the slider bars and can be repositioned by dragging the light icon around. If you add too many lights accidently, just press the **Delete/Backspace** button on your keyboard to remove them.

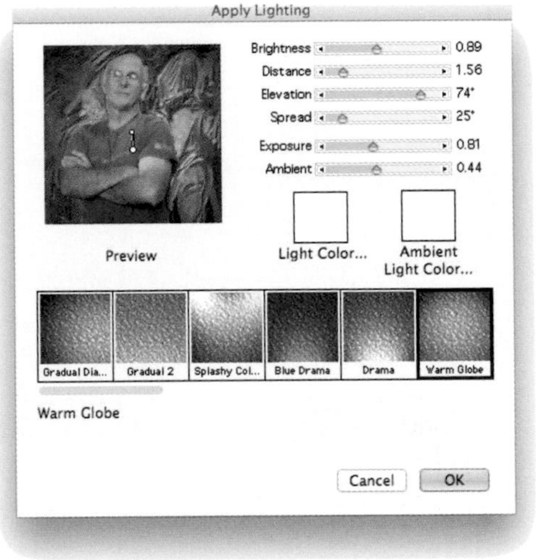

Figure 5.19 Got a light?

Source: Corel ® Corporation. Art © 2014 Cengage Learning.

Figure 5.20 Acrylic graffiti.

© 2014 Cengage Learning.

Create additional contrast between the figure and the background by changing the color scheme of the clone source (the original photo). Use the **Underpainting** panel from the **Autopainting** group and choose the **Impressionist Color Scheme**. The result is higher saturation of colors and a shift to green, as shown in Figure 5.21.

Figure 5.21 A hint of mint.

© 2014 Cengage Learning.

Load the selection once again, and you're ready to work on the figure. As soon as you attempt to make a stroke, the dialog shown in Figure 5.22 comes up, giving you three options. You can create a new source image with the **Impressionist Color** effect, keeping the original source image untouched. "Update" means that the color change will be applied to the original source image. Finally, you can choose to undo the color change. I picked the **Create New** option, so I now have two clone sources, as shown in Figure 5.23.

Figure 5.22 Proceed with caution.

Source: Corel ® Corporation.

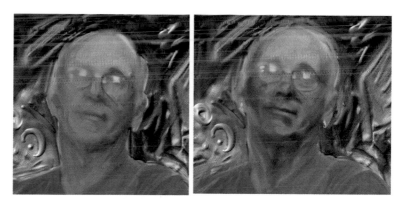

Figure 5.23 Two kinds of Kens.

Source: Corel ® Corporation. Art © 2014 Cengage Learning.

Choose the **Oil Brush Cloner** and add it to your custom palette. This brush variant provides a realistic oil paint effect when you use strokes that follow the contours of Ken's face, arms, and t-shirt. The left side of Figure 5.24 shows several **Oil Brush Cloner** strokes on Ken's face. The version on the right is the result of another color change made to the Clone Soure. To intensify contrast and get some darker shadows, I applied the **Adjust Color** effect to the current clone source, reducing the Value (Brightness) setting. The finished painting of Ken is shown in Figure 5.25.

Figure 5.24 Ken again.

© 2014 Cengage Learning.

Figure 5.25
Ready to print on canvas.

© 2014 Cengage Learning.

Funny Faces

I've been using Painter to create live caricature at events for more than 20 years. Here's your chance to try your hand at distorting facial features to get a humorous likeness. Open **emily_profile.jpg**, shown in Figure 5.26. Your goal is to capture the essence of Emily's face and its expression. The first thing I notice when I start on Emily is her wonderful head of corkscrew curls. I will enjoy making the most of it.

Figure 5.26 Emily and her hair.

© 2014 Cengage Learning.

Simplify and Exaggerate

My basic custom palette for creating a caricature is shown in Figure 5.27.

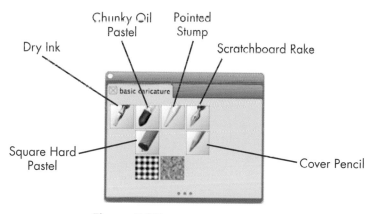

Dry Ink

Chunky Oil Pastel

Pointed Stump

Scratchboard Rake

Square Hard Pastel

Cover Pencil

Figure 5.27 Basic caricature palette.

Source: Corel ® Corporation.

The first stage in Emily's caricature, shown in Figure 5.28, is done with **Dry Ink (Calligraphy** category**)**. This brush makes a bristly line with wide variations in thickness as a function of stylus pressure. It's always 100% opaque and does not show paper grain. I fluffed out her hair and made a long smooth stroke for the neck.

Add a new layer for color, using the **Gel** or **Multiply** method, so the outlines will show through. Fill in a basic skin tone and hair color with **Dry Ink**, for the result shown in Figure 5.29. I plan to use several shades of purple, Emily's favorite color, in her hair.

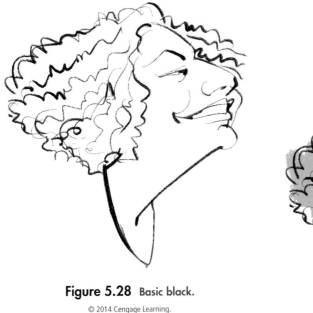

Figure 5.28 Basic black.

© 2014 Cengage Learning.

Figure 5.29 Skin and hair.

© 2014 Cengage Learning.

Life Is Short—Don't Erase!

There is no eraser in this custom palette. However, you can easily remove unwanted pixels by painting with white. (Recall that holding down the **Option/Alt** key while you work switches to the **Dropper** tool.) For tiny corrections, use the **Cover Pencil**. The word "Cover" means that it is capable of covering dark pixels with lighter colors.

Playful Touches

Dab on some rosy cheeks and eye-shadow colors with the **Oil Pastel**. Then blend the edges of colors with the **Pointed Stump**. You can augment Emily's hair with the **Scratchboard Rake**, a timesaving brush for applying several parallel lines at once. My rake strokes are enhanced with **Color Variability** settings that allow each stroke to contain lines that vary by **Hue**, **Saturation**, or **Value** (brightness). Find **Color Variability** controls in the **Brush Control Panels** under the **Window** menu. Figure 5.30 shows this stage in the caricature. Figure 5.31 shows default rake strokes on the left with color varation added to the strokes on the right.

Figure 5.30 Hair and makeup.

© 2014 Cengage Learning.

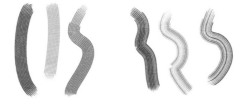

Figure 5.31 Rake and variable rake.

© 2014 Cengage Learning.

Your Very Own Variant

If you want to make your custom changes permanent, create a new variant with your new settings. **Brushes > Save Variant** lets you give the new brush a descriptive name, as shown in Figure 5.32. Add your new variant to the current category or any category you choose.

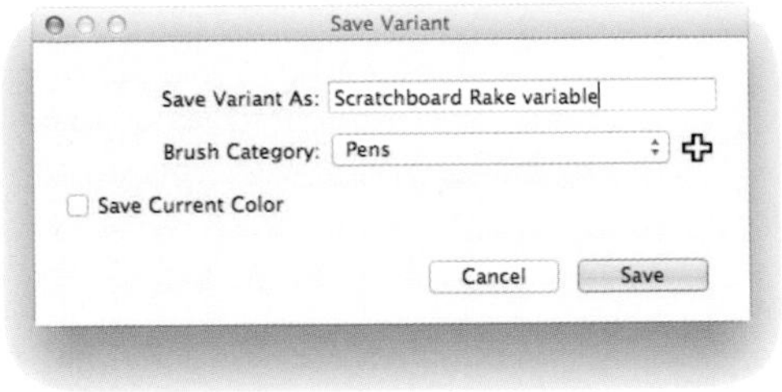

Figure 5.32 New rake in town.

Source: Corel ® Corporation.

Figure 5.33 shows the finished caricature of Emily, with colors blended, highlights added with **Oil Pastel**, and the **Scratchboard Rake** used to create glamorous eyelashes. A few strokes with **Dry Ink** make a background of contrasting color.

Figure 5.33 Emily finished.

© 2014 Cengage Learning.

What's Next?

You have completed the basic lessons in digital painting and had a peek at a few advanced techniqes. Still to come are an examination of Brush Control variables. You'll continue to explore Painter's features more deeply. I'll reveal some of the hidden treasures of this program, but I'll allow others to remain hidden.

You may already have some favorite Painter brushes and tools. Are you developing a style of your own? Consider working in a range of styles, choosing among them when you begin a new project.

Beyond the Basics

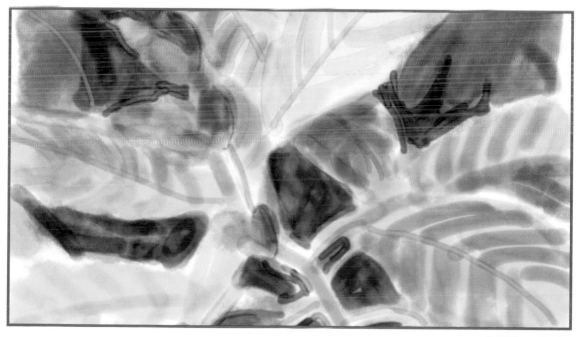

6 Everything's Under Control

This lesson is devoted to helping you create your very own unique Painter environment. You will learn to customize your brushes, art materials, and workspace. I saved this discussion for the middle of the book because I wanted to let you get the feel of Painter X3 before getting too technical.

You've already begun using many of Painter's customizing features, like grouping brushes into custom palettes and setting the sensitivity of tablet pressure with Brush Tracking. If you worked all the previous lessons, you know how to create a new icon for items in a custom palette, how to make a new paper texture, and how to save a new variant in the Brush library. If you've been skipping around, I'll cover most of that stuff here, too.

For this lesson you'll use

• **Images:** rasa_birthday.jpg, art_shoes.jpg

What's Your Preference?

Setting preferences is the first step in managing Painter's behavior. You'll find them in a drop-down menu when you click on **Corel Painter X3** at the top of your computer screen. The default settings are fine for most situations, but by now you know some of the options you prefer. I'm inclined to accept the factory settings for **General Preferences**. The **Interface** section, shown in Figure 6.1, is another story.

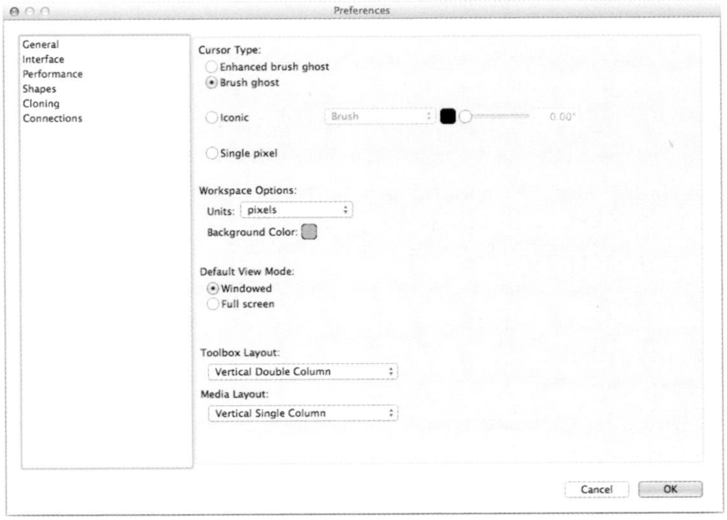

Figure 6.1 Interface time.

Source: Corel ® Corporation.

Your choice of the **Cursor Type** is an important decision, because you'll be looking at it constantly while you draw and paint. If you choose an iconic cursor, such as a triangle or a tiny cartoon paintbrush, you can determine its angle and color. My preference is for **Brush Ghost**, an outline of the current brush tip. This gives me information about the size and shape of the brush as I'm using it. A single pixel is precise but too hard to see, especially at my age. **Enhanced Brush Ghost** shows you the angle of your Wacom stylus, in case you really don't know, but it's a memory hog.

Workspace Units are pixels by default, and it's a good idea to get used to that. I'm finally giving up relying on inches. But I do insist that my temperature be taken in Fahrenheit. For **View Mode**, choose **Windowed** if you want easy access to everything else on your desktop, or **Full Screen** to eliminate distractions. **Toolbox Layout** can be vertical or horizontal, arranged as a double or a single column. I like a vertical double column, so I can see all the tools at a glance, which I use for Photoshop, too. **Media Layout** refers to libraries of **Gradients**, **Patterns**, **Nozzles**, **Looks**, and **Weaves**. The **Paper** library qualifies for a space on the actual **Toolbox**.

Moving on to the **Performance** section, do what you can to optimize speed and efficiency. If you have a secondary drive or partition, use it for the **Scratch Drive**. Consider reducing the **Undo Levels** from the default 32. The **Shapes** section deals with Painter's **Bezier Curve** or vector features. This is where you'll manage **Fills** and **Stokes**, **Anchor Points**, **Handles**, and **Wings**. Painter **Preferences** has a special section assigned to **Quick Clone** options. By default, all boxes are checked. My preferences are shown in Figure 6.2. I often use **Quick Clone** to simply trace a photo, and I don't need the **Cloner Brushes** for that. I prefer to keep the **Clone Source** image open in any case.

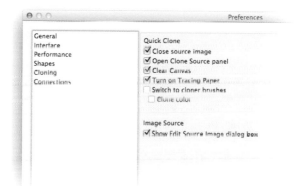

Figure 6.2 Open source.

Source: Corel ® Corporation.

Clone Outsourcing

Painter X3 allows you to choose (via the **Clone Source** panel) any image on your hard drive to function as a clone source, whether it's open or not.

Brush Tracking, shown in Figure 6.3, is found in the **Preferences** menu and is an essential tool for customizing any brush variant to your touch— the pressure and speed of your stroke. Painter X3 will actually remember the setting for individual brush variants! Access Brush Tracking anytime with a handy keyboard shortcut: **Shift+Cmd/Ctrl+, (comma)**. If you like using keyboard shortcuts for actions and commands, you'll find a list in the **Preferences** menu: **Customize Keys**. This section lets you specify custom keys for any menu item.

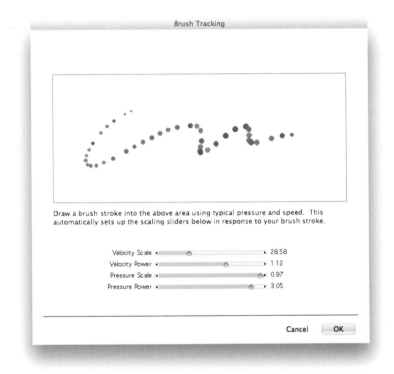

Figure 6.3 Automatically adjusted to you.

Source: Corel ® Corporation.

Pals and Libs

Pal is short for custom palettes, compact little groupings of brushes, media, and commands that you gather together for a specific project or technique. Libs refers to libraries, collections of one kind of media content such as papers, patterns, or gradients.

Let's review the basics of making and managing custom palettes. Begin making a new custom palette by pressing the **Shift** key as you drag a brush variant away from the **Brush Selector**. Figure 6.4 shows the simplest possible custom palette, containing one item, as well as a more complex palette with more brush variants, two paper textures, and a couple of menu commands. The papers were included with the same **Shift**-drag maneuver you use for adding brush variants to the palette. To add a menu command, use **Add Command** from the **Window > Custom Palette** menu. The **Add Command** dialog box, shown in Figure 6.5, prompts you to choose a command and then add it to any open custom palette or start a new palette. The size and shape of the box holding your palette items can be changed by dragging edges or corners in or out. Contents can be shifted around or eliminated by **Shift**-dragging them out of the box.

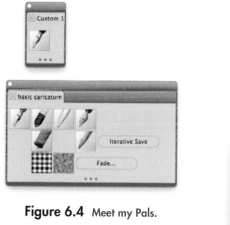

Figure 6.4 Meet my Pals.

Source: Corel ® Corporation.

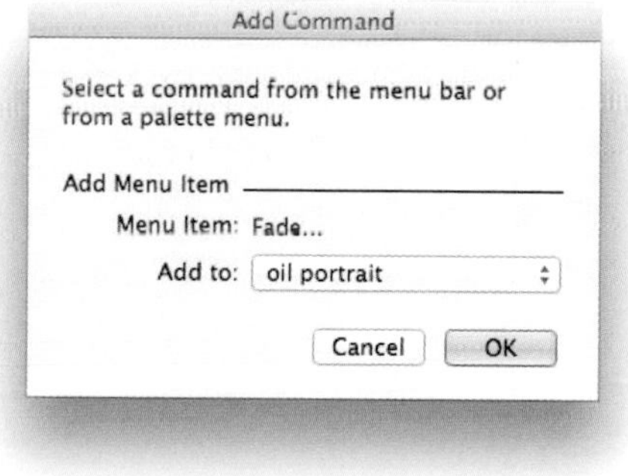

Figure 6.5 I command you!

Source: Corel ® Corporation.

Use the **Custom Palette Organizer**, shown in Figure 6.6, to give your palettes descriptive names and to delete unwanted palettes. The **Import** button allows you to load a custom palette that's not already in your workspace, including those that I've provided for you on the website that supports this book. The **Export** option lets you save any highlighted palette as a file with a PAL file extension.

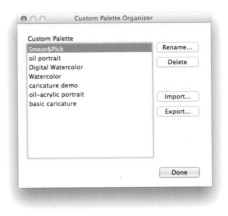

Figure 6.6 Get organized.

Source: Corel ® Corporation.

Iconography

Suppose that you want several brushes from the same category in a custom palette. You'll need a way to tell them apart. Painter X3 makes it easy to change from the default category icon to any other image or simply to the name of the variant. Figure 6.7 shows a custom palette with three variants from the **Pens** category, along with samples of the strokes that each one makes. The **Scratchboard Tool** makes a basic single pen stroke, whereas the **Scratchboard Rake** makes a series of parallel strokes. The "grad" in **Grad Pen** stands for gradient. As you might expect, it paints using colors from the current item in your Gradient Library.

To make an icon out of the actual stroke made by each of the pens

- Drag a tight rectangular selection around a portion of the stroke.

- Right-click (**Ctrl**-click on a Mac) on the corresponding item in your custom palette to get the commands shown in Figure 6.8.

- Choose **Capture Custom Icon**, and your selection instantly replaces the default Pens icon.

Figure 6.7 Three different pens.

Source: Corel ® Corporation.
Art © 2014 Cengage Learning.

Figure 6.8 Icon swap.

Source: Corel ® Corporation.
Art © 2014 Cengage Learning.

Figure 6.9 shows all three icons replaced with the stroke samples. Notice the option at the bottom of the list: **View as Text**. This simply replaces the icon with the name of the specific variant. It's easier than creating a custom icon, but it's not as colorful.

Virtual Libraries

Collections of brushes or art supplies are called libraries in Painter. It's easy to customize libraries—just drag and drop items from one collection to another. If you want to copy an item (move it to a different library without deleting it from the original group), press the **Option/Alt** key as you drag. Figure 6.10 shows other tools for managing papers. **New Library** opens a blank container that you can drag items into and then export (save) with a descriptive name. **Import** allows you to load other libraries from anywhere on your hard drive. **Capture Paper** is available when you have an active selection in your current image. It makes a repeating grayscale tile of the selection and adds it to the current paper library.

Some of these commands are also available in the pop-up menu, where you'll find **Paper Library View** options for size of the swatches. The other media libraries (**Patterns**, **Gradients**, **Nozzles**, and **Weaves**) have similar controls at the bottom of their panel.

Figure 6.9 New icons.

Source: Corel ® Corporation.
Art © 2014 Cengage Learning.

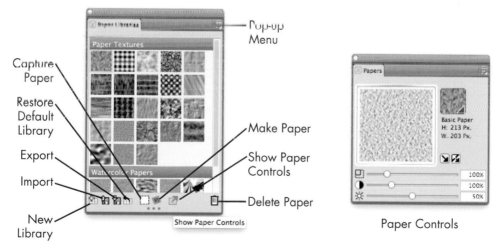

Figure 6.10 Your library card never expires.

Source: Corel ® Corporation.

Happy Media

Not only can you group existing media content any way you wish, but you can make your own original papers, patterns, gradients and other content. For a brief tutorial on capturing paper texture, see the "Paper Work" section in Lesson 4, "The Great Outdoors."

Here's a quick lesson on making a pattern from scratch. Open **rasa_birthday.jpg** and make a tight rectangular selection around one of her eyes, as shown in Figure 6.11. Use the **Capture Pattern** command shown in Figure 6.12. The new pattern takes its place in the current library.

Test your new pattern by painting a few strokes with **Pattern Pen** variants. Figure 6.13 shows strokes made with (from top to bottom) **Pattern Pen**, **Pattern Pen Soft Edge**, and **Pattern Pen Micro**. **Pattern Chalk** and **Pattern Marker** allow you to express the pattern with the current color.

Figure 6.11 Rasa's eye.

© 2014 Cengage Learning.

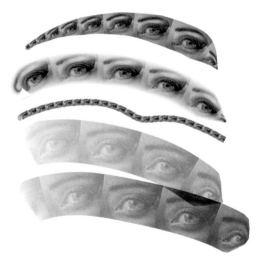

Figure 6.13 The eyes have it.

© 2014 Cengage Learning.

Figure 6.12 Eye is ready.

© 2014 Cengage Learning.

It's so much fun making patterns from images, so let's do one more. Open **art_shoes.jpg**, shown in Figure 6.14. This time select the entire image for the pattern element, and use the **Capture Pattern** command. Make some test strokes once again. Figure 6.15 shows that **Pattern Pen** includes the yellow background, but **Pattern Pen Masked** uses only the shoes and omits the background color.

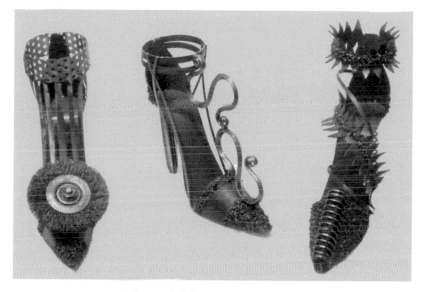

Figure 6.14 Uncomfortable shoes.

© 2014 Cengage Learning.

Figure 6.15 Shoes and masks.

© 2014 Cengage Learning.

Some of the items in the default **Gradient** library, shown in Figure 6.16, are **Spiral** style, others are **Circular**, **Radial**, or **Linear** at various angles. With the **Gradient Control Panel** open, you can switch a gradient to another style, choose a single or double configuration, and change its angle. Spiral gradients provide a control for loosening or tightening the spiral. Two possible configurations are shown for the **Vivid Colored Stripes Gradient**. The top settings are for **Radial**, **Left to Right**. The bottom panel shows **Spiral** with a **Double Right to Left** spin. Adjustments have also been made to the angle and degree of twist.

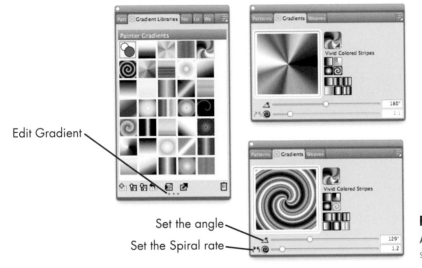

Edit Gradient

Set the angle

Set the Spiral rate

Figure 6.16

Angle, direction, and spin.

Source: Corel ® Corporation.

You can even change the preset colors of a gradient and the way they blend by using the **Edit Gradient** controls. Make some changes to **Water Lily Flower**, whose default color ramp is shown in Figure 6.17. Delete some of the color control points for a smoother blend or to eliminate some colors. Add a new color by clicking inside the **Color Ramp Bar** where you want to place it. A new color control point appears. Assign a color to it as you would choose a color for painting, by choosing from the **Color** panel. My changes are shown in Figure 6.18.

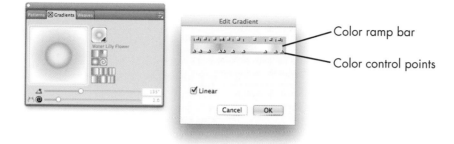

Figure 6.17 Ramp controls.

Source: Corel ® Corporation.

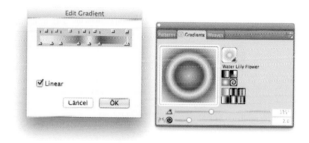

Figure 6.18 Radiant gradient.

Source: Corel ® Corporation.

Gimme Some Space

You've seen what a time-saver it is to have a custom palette for every situation. You can also open and arrange all the panels and tools you'll need for a given project and save the whole layout as a workspace. Get a feel for how some Painter Masters have used this capability by importing some of their workspaces. Then create your own based on an existing workspace, or start one from scratch.

Make Arrangements

A new workspace can take a while to load. It might be quicker to save a palette layout using **Arrange Palettes > Save Layout**.

Total Brush Control

There are 34 separate panels in the **Brush Controls** section of the **Window** menu. You can open all of them at once using the **Cmd/Ctrl+B** keyboard shortcut, or you can choose them individually as needed. Painter X3 introduces an ideal way to access only the controls relevant for your current brush. This dandy feature is called **Advanced Brush Controls**, and its icon appears at the extreme right of your **Property Bar** when the **Brush** tool is active.

For example, the left side of Figure 6.19 shows the **Advanced Brush Controls** panel group that appears when you are using the **Dry Ink** variant of **Calligraphy**. The other group of panels presents itself when you use the **New Simple Water** variant of the **Digital Watercolor** category. Notice that some control panels are sharing the same space. This is an efficient way to limit the amount of desktop "real estate" eaten up by control panels. Click on any gray tab to reveal the choices provided. Consider spending a rainy afternoon fiddling around with various controls on several brush variants to see how your changes affect the brush stroke. You can revert to the default settings by clicking on the **Reset** tool at the extreme left of the **Property Bar**.

Help!

I will discuss just a fraction of the vast number of brush controls. Complete details on this topic and anything else you want to know about Painter X3 are available at your fingertips. Just click on **Help** at the top of your screen and scroll down to **User Guide**. Find what you want in the index, or use the search field to pin down the exact item you want to learn about.

Figure 6.19 Dry or wet.

Source: Corel ® Corporation.

Choose **Dull Conte 22** from the **Conte** category. Traditional French conte "crayons" are slim sticks with a square cross-section. They are similar to oil pastels but have a creamier feel. They typically come in various shades of brown or reddish brown. Make a few strokes, like those shown in Figure 6.20. When you use a lighter color over a darker tone, the lighter one covers it. The two strokes on the left were made with **Basic Paper**, and it's difficult to see the grain. The stroke on the right uses **Linen Canvas**, and the grain is now apparent. Open the **General** controls, shown in Figure 6.21, along with the **Dab Preview**.

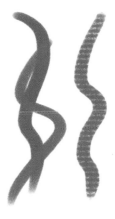

Figure 6.20 Cover and grain.

© 2014 Cengage Learning.

Figuro 6.21 Cuplured dab.

Source: Corel ® Corporation.

The essential structure of a variant is revealed in the **General** control panel. The **Dab Type** for the conte stick is **Captured**, meaning it is the result of selecting an image element: in this case, an oval with random light and dark pixels that look a bit spongy. The **Method** is **Cover**—hence the ability of conte to cover dark strokes with lighter ones. The word **"Grainy"** in the **Subcategory** allows conte to show paper texture. Figure 6.22 shows the dramatic change in conte's behavior when you switch the method from **Cover** to **Buildup**. The opaque yellow stroke on the left was made with conte's default settings. On the right is the same color, but in **Buildup** the variant acts like a marker—transparent and getting darker (building up opacity) with each stroke.

Figure 6.22 Method change.

© 2014 Cengage Learning.

Custom Brushes

Create a new brush variant with a captured dab. First, choose **Round Tip Pen 20** and make a few test squiggles. This variant has a **Circular Dab** type, which you will replace with a cross-hatch element. The cross-hatch was made with two stokes of the **Coit Pen 3**, a **Rake** type variant with three parallel striations. Make a tight rectangular selection of the cross-hatch element, and then return to the **Round Tip Pen**. In the **Brushes** menu, choose **Capture Dab**, and then test your new brush. Figure 6.23 shows the original **Round Tip Pen** squiggles, the captured dab, and strokes made with the new pen.

Figure 6.23 New brush.

© 2014 Cengage Learning.

If you like the quirky, edgy look of this variant, as I do, use the **Save Variant** command in the **Brushes** menu. Figure 6.24 shows the **Save Variant** dialog, where you can give your new brush a descriptive name and choose a category. You can even make a new category for your custom brushes. The category name appears at the bottom of the **Brush Selector** list, with the icon shown in Figure 6.25.

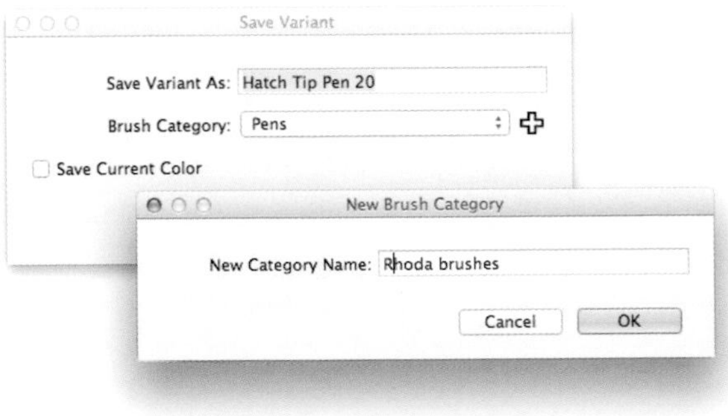

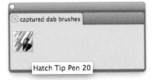

Figure 6.25 Custom palette for custom brushes.

Source: Corel ® Corporation.

Figure 6.24 New category.

Source: Corel ® Corporation.

Switch to the **Thick Opaque Acrylic 30** variant and notice that its **Dab Type** is **Static Bristle**. The **Dab Profile** shown in Figure 6.26 shows numerous bristles, as you would expect. Open the **Static Bristle** control panel, also shown. Experiment with changes in the **Thickness**, **Clumpiness**, and **Hair Scale**. Can you predict how changes will affect the stroke? As you move the sliders, the **Dab and Stroke Previews** update. Figure 6.27 shows how settings influence the look of this bristle brush. The stroke on the left is made with default settings. The center stroke shows reduction of Thickness to 25%, and it seems light and fluffy. The stroke on the right has **Hair Scale** increased to the maximum, for a somewhat sticky look.

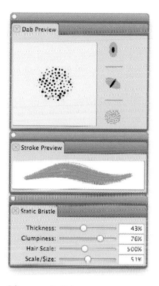

Figure 6.26 A bristly dab.

Source: Corel ® Corporation.

Figure 6.27 Bristly, fluffy, and sticky.

© 2014 Cengage Learning.

Check Your Oils?

Figure 6.28 shows squiggles made with several brushes in the **Artists' Oils** category. To experiment with these variants, make a custom palette as shown in Figure 6.29. Replace each identical icon with the name of the brush by choosing **View as Text** after you right-click the icon (**Ctrl**-click on the Mac).

Figure 6.29 Custom oils palette.

Source: Corel ® Corporation.

Figure 6.28 Oily strokes.

© 2014 Cengage Learning.

What makes these variants run out of paint? Open the **Artists' Oils** control panel, shown in Figure 6.30, and notice, among other settings, the **Trail-off** slider. Let's test the theory that changing the **Trail-off** amount will influence how quickly the stroke dries up.

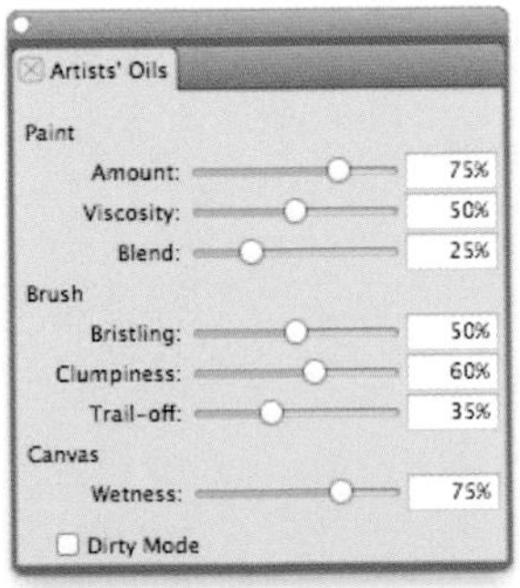

Figure 6.30 Oily sliders.

Source: Corel ® Corporation.

It does not appear to work. Let's look at some of the other variables and guess which ones might have an effect. Reduce the **Amount** of paint, and you have success. Likewise, increasing the **Viscosity** of the paint results in drying out more quickly. Various combinations of those two variables give you complete control of **Trail-off**, as shown in Figure 6.31. I'm not sure what the actual **Trail-off** setting does.

Detective Work

Descriptions about brush controls in the online **Help** section are useful, but it's more effective (and more fun) to investigate on your own by changing settings and testing the results.

Figure 6.31 Happy Trail-offs to you.

© 2014 Cengage Learning.

What's Next?

You're now armed with enough information about **Brush Controls** to explore more of them with confidence. You'll have plenty of chances to work with that knowledge elsewhere in the book. In the next lesson, you'll learn all about Painter's **Text** tool and how to do tricks with type. You'll also have a chance to play with some extraordinary special effects.

7 Texts and Effects

This lesson is mostly about letterforms and Painter's capacity to provide you with a wide range of graphic ways to create and alter them. Painter has various options for text effects. Many of these special effects can go way beyond the alphabet and be applied to images of all kinds.

By the time you finish this lesson, you'll be able to write with liquid metal, melted chocolate, flowers, or bits of gravel. You'll learn to skew and distort letters, burn their edges, and fill them with gradients, patterns, and photos.

For this lesson you'll use

- **Images:** sunset1.jpg, SansSouci-Potsdam.jpg, Berlin_wall.jpg, Leipzig_new-university.jpg, chocolate_icing1.jpg, chocolate_icing2.jpg

Texting

Painter's **Text** tool icon is a capital letter **T**. When it is active, the **Property Bar** gives you many of the standard choices for font, point size, and alignment that you expect in a word processing or page layout application. You can choose to have a drop shadow or an interior shadow applied automatically as you enter text. There are separate color and opacity controls as well as composite method choices for how the text and its shadow interact with layers below them. Just highlight **Text Attributes** or **Shadow Attributes** to alter them independently. Figure 7.1 gets you acquainted with these options. When you click on your canvas with the **Text** tool, a special layer is automatically created, and the first few words you type appear in the **Layer** panel.

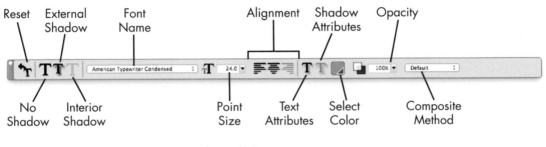

Figure 7.1 This is only a text.

Source: Corel ® Corporation.

The **Text** panel, shown in Figure 7.2, gives you most of the **Property Bar** choices and a few more controls. Here's where you'll adjust *tracking* (letter spacing) and *leading* (the spacing between lines of text) and assign a curve style. You can independently assign blur effects at the bottom of the palette to the text and shadow.

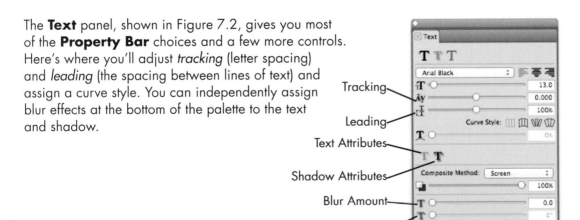

Figure 7.2 "Leading" rhymes with wedding.

Source: Corel ® Corporation.

The text in Figure 7.3 was made with a typeface called Arial Black. The top sample has a crisp drop shadow. The second variation has a drop shadow with a directional blur of 290 degrees. I reduced the tracking value to squeeze the letters closer together. The bottom sample uses the **Screen Composite Method** for the text and a blur value of 12 for the shadow. There is less space between the two lines because of a lower leading amount. With so many possible variations, we may never know if the fox finally jumps over that dang dog.

The quick brown fox...

The quick brown fox...

The quick brown fox...

Figure 7.3 Me and my shadows.

© 2014 Cengage Learning.

Vacation Postcard

Did you create a Hawaiian sunset graphic in Lesson 4, "The Great Outdoors"? If so, open it now. If not, just open the original **sunset1.jpg** image shown in Figure 7.4.

Figure 7.4 Wish I were here.

© 2014 Cengage Learning.

Let's add the word "Aloha!" to the image. Rummage around for a font that conveys the tropical splendor of the island. Figure 7.5 shows a few likely possibilities. From top to bottom, they are Lithos Pro Black, Stoney Billy, Papyrus Condensed, and Hot Coffee.

Figure 7.5 Do these fonts make me look fat?

© 2014 Cengage Learning.

Got Fonts?

Type **Aloha!** on the image, using your font of choice. I'll work with Lithos Pro Black. Rather than using the point size slider in the **Property Bar**, which can be difficult to control, switch to the **Layer Adjuster** tool. You'll see the tiny hollow square handles for scaling any item. Drag a handle or two to get the size you want, and notice that you can distort the proportions if needed. Drag from inside the text to move it into position. Figure 7.6 shows the lettering with a softly blurred drop shadow and a ribbon style curve.

Figure 7.6 Put the HA! back into Aloha.

© 2014 Cengage Learning.

fonts of Wisdom

It's unlikely you'll have the same fonts on your hard drive that I use in this project. Find a substitute that pleases you. Mistral is a standard font that works well for this project. Several font houses are included in the resources at the back of the book. They provide low-cost typefaces for all occasions.

Nice Curves!

Creating text on a curve in Painter requires some new skills. After you apply a curve style, you can change the curve of the path. You'll use Bézier curves, meaning that the shape of the baseline can be manipulated using control handles and anchor points. Choose the **Shape Selector** tool and try changing the positions of the anchor points and the length and direction of the handles until you can maneuver the curve into the shape you want. The "Aloha!" at the top of Figure 7.7 shows the **Curve Ribbon** before you edit it. After some experimenting, shown in the center, the bottom text is pretty close to the look desired.

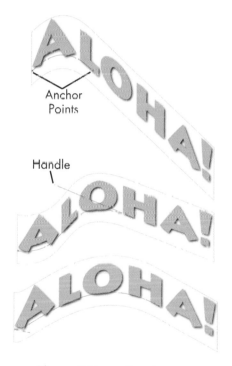

Anchor Points

Handle

Figure 7.7 Handling the curves.

© 2014 Cengage Learning.

Handles and Points

Although Painter is pixel based, it does provide a few powerful vector-based tools. (See the Appendix, "Fundamentals and Beyond," for a fuller explanation.) The **Shape Selector** and the **Pen** tool (not to be confused with the **Pens** category of brushes!) provide the means for making editable shapes with strokes and fills. With a bit of practice, you can learn to make and edit complex and exact shapes. When you're finished, you have to convert the vector shapes to pixels, or *rasterize* them.

Do you want to create something a bit more interesting than just plain orange lettering? No problem. You can create many exciting effects after you rasterize the text; that is you can convert the text layer to a default image layer. That conversion can be done automatically as soon as you apply brushes or bucket fills to a text layer. The first time you attempt to paint or squirt something on text, the warning shown in Figure 7.8 pops up. If you're sure you don't need to change the curve or the shadows, click **Commit**. If you're pretty sure you don't need to be warned again and again, check the "don't ask" box.

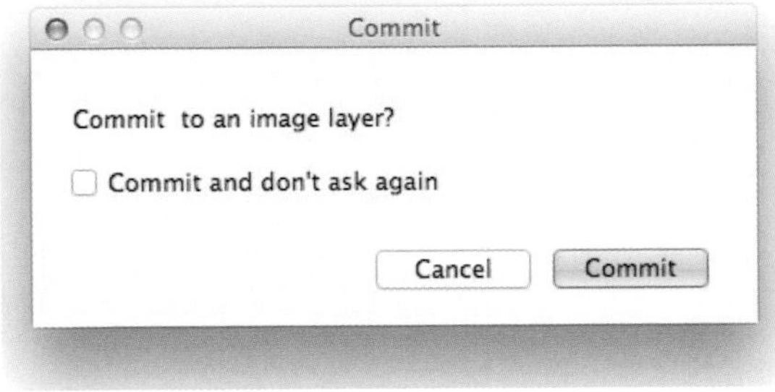

Figure 7.8 Don't ask!

Source: Corel ® Corporation.

Special Effects

Before you commit the text to create the Tropical Leaf pattern fill shown in Figure 7.9, move the shadow farther away from the text. Just highlight **Shadow Attributes** in the **Text** panel and use the **Layer Adjuster** tool to drag the shadow anywhere you want it. Use the **Pattern Pen** (review Lesson 5, "Painting People," if needed), and just touch it to the text to get the **Commit** dialog.

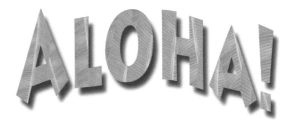

Figure 7.9 Leafy fill.

To get the Tropical Leaf pattern used here, you have to load the **Painter 8 Pattern Library**. Use the **Import** command at the bottom of the **Pattern** control panel, shown in Figure 7.10. Or just use one of the patterns in the default library.

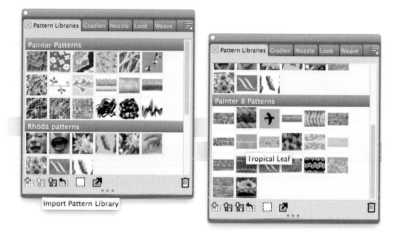

Figure 7.10 Pattern import-export.

Source: Corel ® Corporation.

You're almost ready to paint the tropical leaves into the text. But first, turn on the **Preserve Transparency** feature in the **Layers** panel, shown in Figure 7.11. When the tiny icon with the padlock is blue, your strokes will affect only the lettering and not the transparent background of the layer. Look carefully on the "Aloha!" layer to see the gray-and-white checkerboard indicating transparency. Okay, now you can paint the lettering with **Pattern Pen** or **Pattern Pen Masked**.

Figure 7.11 Transparency lock-down.

Source: Corel ® Corporation.

Art © 2014 Cengage Learning.

The effect in Figure 7.12 is a **Paint Bucket** gradient fill, with the appropriately named **Summer Sunset** gradient. (Although it was January when I took the photo, it felt like summer.) The only prepration necessary here is to use the **Drop and Select** command in the **Layers** panel menu. The marching ants selection is visible in this figure.

It's fun to sprinkle palm trees on the lettering, as shown in Figure 7.13.

Figure 7.12 Sunset fill.

© 2014 Cengage Learning.

Figure 7.13 Palm tree sprinkles.

© 2014 Cengage Learning.

Allow me to introduce you to the **Image Hose** category of brushes. These variants spray tiny images that you load from the **Nozzle** library, shown in Figure 7.14. The actual variants instruct the hose how to deposit images. The basic choices are **Linear** and **Spray**. The controllers include Pressure **(P)**, Direction **(D)**, and Random **(R)**.

Figure 7.14 Nozzles for every occasion!

Source: Corel ® Corporation.

Open a new blank image to play around with the **Image Hose**. Figure 7.15 shows (from the top):

- **Red Poppies** nozzle, **Linear-Size-P**

- **Red Poppies** nozzle, **Spray-Size-R**

- **Swallows** nozzle, **Linear-Size-R**

- **Swallows** nozzle, **Spray-Size-P Angle-D**

Load the **Palm Trees** nozzle and use the **Spray-Size-R** variant to sprinkle some trees on the "Aloha!" layer.

Figure 7.15 Flowers and birds.

Source: Corel ® Corporation.

More Text Tricks

Some **Image Hose** nozzles can be used for handwritten words that are self-descriptive. Spray some **Concrete** or **Stucco** on a new canvas. Then load the **Dirt** nozzle and switch to a **Linear** variant to write the word "dirt." Use the **Stone Wall** nozzle from the Painter 11 library to write the word "stone." Finish it off with an ampersand made with the **Gravel** nozzle for the graphic shown in Figure 7.16. Now go wash your hands.

Figure 7.16 Quick and dirty signage.

© 2014 Cengage Learning.

Travel Poster

The dramatic image in Figure 7.17 combines the name of a historically important German city with a photo of one of its most famous landmarks. Open the photo **SansSouci-Potsdam.jpg**, shown in Figure 7.18.

Figure 7.17 A peek at Potsdam.

© 2014 Cengage Learning.

Figure 7.18 The Sans Souci pavilion.

© 2014 Cengage Learning.

Choose a bold typeface, such as those shown in Figure 7.19. The top font is **Impact**, and the other two are **Gill Sans Ultra Bold**. The bottom sample is more condensed, the result of simply squeezing the text closer together with the **Layer Adjuster** tool.

Type **potsdam** as large as possible on the Sans Souci photo, as shown in Figure 7.20. It's important to use black, as you'll soon see. A new Text layer was created automatically. You'll need to get the type to go under the photo by using this cut-and-paste maneuver.

1. With the **Canvas** highlighted, choose **Select > All (Cmd/Ctrl+A)**.

2. Choose **Edit > Cut (Cmd/Ctrl+X)**.

3. Choose **Edit > Paste (Cmd/Ctrl+V)**.

Figure 7.19 Bold and condensed.

© 2014 Cengage Learning.

Figure 7.20 Black letters.

© 2014 Cengage Learning.

You have successfully created the layered arrangement shown in Figure 7.21. The photo completely hides the text until you switch the composite method to **Lighten**.

Enlightenment

Here's what happens when you use **Lighten** mode on the top (photo) layer. Comparing the two layers, **Painter** reveals whichever pixels are lighter. So the white background around the text wins over the photo, and the photo wins over the black text.

Figure 7.21 Photo fills text.

Source: Corel ® Corporation.
Art © 2014 Cengage Learning.

Adding a drop shadow to the lettering takes a bit more work, now that the letters have been converted to a default layer. You'll need to separate the letters from the white background. Just use the **Magic Wand** to click on all the white areas (don't forget to **Shift**-click on the enclosed white spaces of the letters). Then choose **Select > Invert Selection**, so that the letters are the active selection, and use a copy-and-paste sequence to put the work on its own layer. Finally, use **Effects > Objects > Create Drop Shadow**, accepting the default settings. The result is a shadow that you can manipulate independently of the lettering. Figure 7.22 shows your **Layers** panel at this point with the layer and its shadow as a group. Spin the triangle to open the group so you can have access to the shadow. Move it down and to the right a few pixels with the **Layer Adjuster** tool.

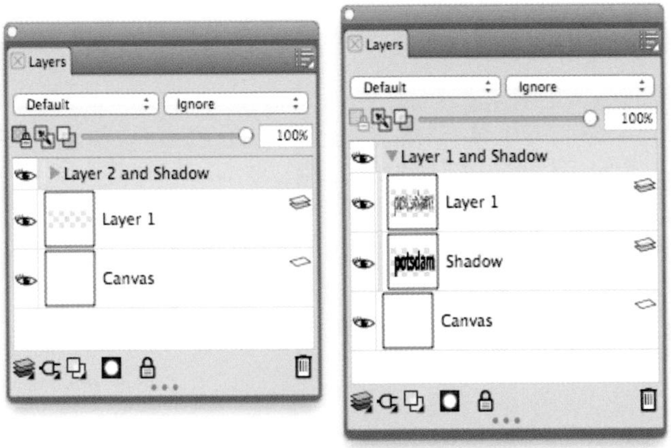

Figure 7.22 The Shadow knows.

Source: Corel ® Corporation.

Use the same steps to create composites using the **Leipzig_new-university.jpg** and **Berlin_wall.jpg** photos, shown in Figure 7.23. Then arrange all three composites into a travel poster with the caption, "Visit Germany!" Choose an elegant script such as Zapfino, shown in Figure 7.24. Rotate a layer using **Edit > Transform > Rotate**, or use the **Transform** tool in the **Toolbox** (sharing a space with the **Layer Adjuster**). Drop all layers to save as a JPEG or other file format. This could be one of several designs featuring different European countries.

Figure 7.23 Who's that tourist?

© 2014 Cengage Learning.

Figure 7.24 Show us your passport.

© 2014 Cengage Learning.

Distressed Text

Here's a way to make text look rusted and eroded. Type the word **rusty** in any suitable font with black for the text color. I'm using Impact. Load an **Image Hose** variant with the **Rust** nozzle, and enable **Preserve Transparency** in the **Layers** panel. Then spray the layer to completely fill the text, but leave the white background unchanged. The original text and the rust-filled version are shown in Figure 7.25.

Figure 7.25 My typing is a bit rusty.

© 2014 Cengage Learning.

Eroding the edges of the letters requires another effect.

1. Use the **Drop** command in the **Layers** menu.

2. Click the **Magic Wand** tool on a white pixel to select them all.

3. Choose **Select > Invert Selection**, so only the rusty letters are active.

4. Choose **Cut (Cmd/Ctrl+X)** and **Paste (Cmd/Ctrl+V)** to delete the rusty letters from the canvas and put them on a layer.

And now, welcome to the amazing **Dynamic** plug-ins! They are found at the bottom of the **Layers** panel (also in the **Layers** menu) and have an electric plug icon. Choose **Burn**, and adjust settings in the dialog box shown in Figure 7.26. Your settings will depend on the size and font you use and how much erosion you desire.

Burn Options

Burn Margin	5%
Flame Breadth	8%
Flame Strength	27%
Wind Direction	-56
Wind Strength	0%
Jaggedness	50%

☐ Use paper texture
☑ Burn interior edges
☑ Preview
☐ Off

Burn Color...

Save As Default   Reset   Cancel   OK

Figure 7.26 A burning sensation.

The final stage, shown in Figure 7.27, also has a drop shadow. This is made using a method quite different from creating an external shadow with the **Text** tool. **Effects > Objects > Create Drop Shadow** provides settings for offset, opacity, and a couple of other variables, but not color. Accept the default values and click **OK**.

Figure 7.27 Rusted type.

Figure 7.28 shows your **Layers** panel at this point, with the shadow on its own layer, grouped with the original layer. Spin the triangle to open the group so you can work on the shadow separately. You can change its color now. Select only the **Shadow** layer, and turn on the **Preserve Transparency** function. (It's blue when active.) This ensures that only the shadow pixels are changed. Pick a dark reddish brown and choose the **Paint Bucket** tool, with **Current Color** in the **Fill With** field on the **Property Bar**. When you pour current color with the **Paint Bucket**, the shadow becomes rusty, too. Handle with care, or you might need a tetanus shot.

Figure 7.28 Shadow sold separately.

Source: Corel ® Corporation.

A Cocoa Logo (Back by Popular Demand)

My recipe for writing with melted chocolate was such a huge hit in the previous edition that I'll serve it up again, with some variations.

Make a fresh new canvas that will fit comfortably on your screen at 100% size, and visit the **Dynamic** plug ins again. Choose **Liquid Metal** this time. Figure 7.29 shows the **Liquid Metal** controls, which must remain open while you work.

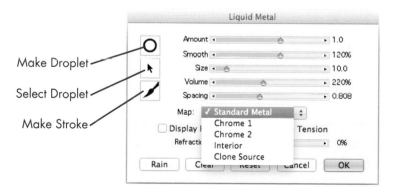

Figure 7.29 Hot metal controls.

Source: Corel ® Corporation.

Practice making strokes with the brush, and switch to the circle to make metallic droplets. Notice the tendency for droplets to attract each other and run together. The **Undo** command won't work here, so if you want to remove a stroke or a droplet, use the arrow icon to select it and then press the **Delete/Backspace** key. You can even use the arrow to drag a rectangular selection around larger areas to delete all the contained strokes or drops at once. Strokes are actually made up of a sequence of droplets. You can see them individually by enabling **Display Handles**. Figure 7.30 shows droplets and strokes.

Figure 7.30 Metallic drops and strokes.

© 2014 Cengage Learning.

The choice you make in the **Map** field determines the reflections on the strokes and drops. Changes will have a dramatic effect. Notice that **Clone Source** is one of the alternatives to the default **Standard Metal** in the list. With a little tweaking of the controls and preparing alternate source images for the reflection map, you can emulate a variety of liquids, including melted chocolate! Click **OK** or **Cancel** to dismiss the Liquid Metal controls.

Consider the Source

Suppose you don't have an image designated as a clone source. Painter then uses the current pattern as the "default" clone source.

In Lesson 6, "Everything's Under Control," you created new patterns by capturing a selection in an image. You'll do the same with each of the chocolate_icing photos. Make a large rectangular selection on the dark chocolate image and open the **Patterns** control panel, shown in Figure 7.31.

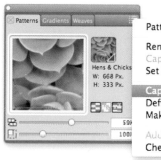

Figure 7.31 Create a new pattern.

Source: Corel ® Corporation.

Use the **Capture Pattern** command with the settings shown in Figure 7.32, and you will instantly have a dark chocolate pattern added to the current library. A **Paint Bucket** fill with this pattern is shown in Figure 7.33. Repeat the **Capture Pattern** steps with the milk chocolate version.

Figure 7.32 Instant chocolate.

Source: Corel ® Corporation. Art © 2014 Cengage Learning.

Figure 7.33 Chocolate filling.

© 2014 Cengage Learning.

Open a fresh **Liquid Metal** plug-in layer. Write **cocoa** with **Liquid Metal** strokes, using **Clone Source** for the reflection map. Figure 7.34 shows the lettering with each of the chocolate sources. I increased the refraction setting for the dark chocolate version to 15% to brighten it up a bit.

Let's make the letters more interesting by dragging some droplets around with the arrow tool. The drippy version, shown in Figure 7.35, is more convincing and more delicious. Delete any extra droplets you don't want. In real life, you could simply eat them.

Figure 7.34 Plain chocolate.

© 2014 Cengage Learning.

Figure 7.35 How sweet…and bittersweet.

© 2014 Cengage Learning.

What's Next?

Do you need to take a break for a real cup of cocoa or chocolate treat? If you were really into that last project, you might need to jog around the block a couple of times to lower your blood sugar.

In the next lesson, we'll get back to fine art drawing and painting projects.

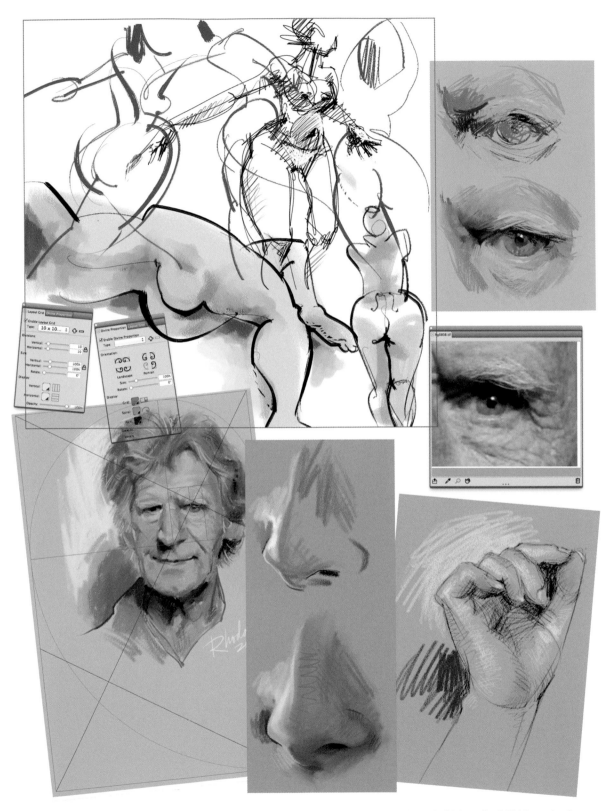

8 Life Drawing

If you have studied drawing in a traditional way, it's a good bet that you did some life drawing, working with nude models. Studying the human figure is an excellent way to learn how to observe natural forms and transform them into two-dimensional lines, shapes, and tones on paper or canvas. Mastery of the skills needed to draw the figure with correct proportions, especially the head and hands, can take many years. This section will either get you started down that road or help you get to the next rest stop.

For this lesson you'll use

- **Images:** Several photos in the People, Figure Drawing, Heads, and Face Parts folders

Hand Made

You won't have to hire a professional artist's model to begin working from life. You can start by drawing your own hand—the one not holding your stylus. The human hand is capable of a vast number of positions and expressions. Figure 8.1 shows just a few of them. Once you start adding props like spoons or finger cymbals, the possibilities increase exponentially!

The external structure and proportions of the hand will require close observation. Improving your ability to sketch hands will pay off when you create portrait drawings or figure studies later in this lesson.

Figure 8.1 Need a hand?

© 2014 Cengage Learning.

Make a custom palette composed of the brush variants shown in Figure 8.2.

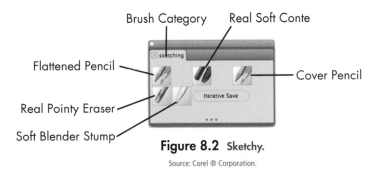

Figure 8.2 Sketchy.

Source: Corel ® Corporation.

Make some scribbles and crosshatching with the two pencils and the conte stick to get the feel for them. Figure 8.3 shows strokes made with dark brown and a creamy pink color. You'll use these two colors for your sketch, so keep them handy. Scribbles on the left were made with the **Flattened Pencil**, center strokes show **Real Soft Conte** stick marks, and the delicate lines on the right were done with **Cover Pencil**. **Real Soft Conte** and **Cover Pencil** allow you to cover dark strokes with lighter ones. That is the beauty of the **Cover Method** in determining the behavior of brushes. Marks made with the **Flattened Pencil** can only get darker; that tool uses the **Buildup Method**. (See Lesson 6, "Everything's Under Control," for more about controlling brush behavior).

Let's warm up with the photo in Figure 8.4.

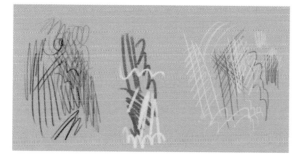

Figure 8.3 My two-year old can do that!

© 2014 Cengage Learning.

Figure 8.4 A feminine touch.

© 2014 Cengage Learning.

Create a new blank canvas with a warm gray or buff paper color. Use dark brown to block out the basic shapes with light strokes of the **Flattened Pencil**. Add more definition and darker values in the shadows and creases. Figure 8.5 shows these stages in the drawing. Use the dark "negative shapes" between fingers and thumb to make corrections as you work. If you need to tilt the canvas to work more comfortably, use the **Rotate Page** tool.

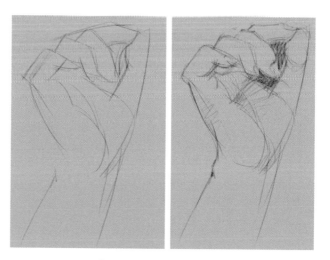

Figure 8.5 Hand crafting.

© 2014 Cengage Learning.

Allow the paper color to work as the mid-tone and add a few highlights in cream. The finished sketch is shown in Figure 8.6. Practice sketching your own hand in various poses, with and without props, with directional lighting to emphasize contrast. When you get tired of your own hand, use the other photos in the **Hands** folder.

Practice Your Fingering

Your fingers are not cylindrical, like sausages (unless you have really let yourself go)! They are more like a string of boxcars. You can see that more clearly when your fingers are slightly curled.

Figure 8.6 A big hand for the little lady.

© 2014 Cengage Learning.

Heads Up

In preparation for drawing or painting a portrait from "scratch"—that is, without cloning or tracing—it will be very helpful to learn a few guidelines about the proportions of the head and facial features. Notice the relative dimensions and relationships shown in Figure 8.7.

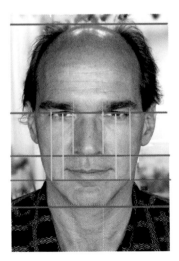

Figure 8.7 Face facts.

© 2014 Cengage Learning.

The horizontal lines in red show that the distance from the top of Barry's head to his eyes is the same as the distance from his eyes to his chin. The eyes-to-chin dimension is halved at the base of his nose, and the nose-to-chin length is equally divided at the bottom of the lip. For some vertical measurements, notice that the space between the eyes is about the same as the width of each eye. The tear ducts of the eyes line up with the wings of the nostrils. The centers of the pupils should line up with the corners of the mouth.

Of course, there are individual variations due to ethnicity, gender, and age, but the proportions are remarkably consistent. Noticing slight deviations from the average will help you capture a likeness, rather than a generic-looking face.

The Eyes Have It

Practice drawing individual features before you attempt to put them together. Let's start at the top and work down. Practice using the eye chart shown in Figure 8.8. This composite is available in the **People > Face Parts** folder.

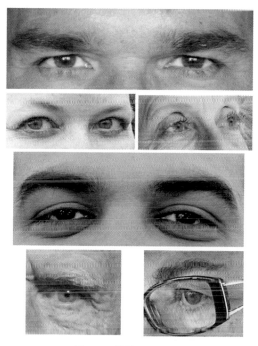

Figure 8.8 Eyes front.

© 2014 Cengage Learning.

Eyes Right

The eyeball is a sphere, so its curvature must be described by darker shading near both corners. A shadow between the eye and bridge of the nose is created by the eye socket. The "shelf" of the lower eyelid tends to catch light, while the upper lid (and sometimes the brow ridge) casts a shadow over the top of the eyeball. There is a slight bulge below the eye, to accommodate the lower part of the eyeball. In addition to a shiny spot on the pupil, there may be tiny highlights visible in the lachrymal gland, and the wet line where the eyeball meets the lower eyelid.

Make a new image with a tinted paper color, as you did for your sketch of the hand. Try a different tint this time. You'll make a detailed color rendering, using the custom palette shown in Figure 8.9. These dry media variants are members of three different categories. They all use the **Cover** method and work well together for drawings that suggest traditional pastels or charcoal. Make some practice strokes with all three as well as the **Smudge** tool.

Soft Pastel   Charcoal Pencil

Grainy Cover Pencil —

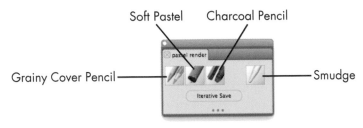

— Smudge

Figure 8.9 Dry media.

Source: Corel ® Corporation.

Load the eye chart as a Reference Image and scroll to Stephen's piercing green eye, as shown in Figure 8.10. Use the **Grainy Cover Pencil** to establish the basic shapes and tones in a dark brown. Switch to either the **Soft Pastel** or the **Charcoal Pencil** to develop the forms with color sampled from the Reference Image. Apply controlled hatches and cross-hatches of color that follow the direction and curves of the eye. Refer to Figure 8.11 to guide you. Blend some edges with the **Smudge** tool, but don't get too smooth. It's important for the viewer to see some of your "brushwork." Return to the **Grainy Cover Pencil** for fine detail and eyebrow hairs.

Figure 8.10 You lookin' at me?

© 2014 Cengage Learning.

Figure 8.11 Eye shadowed.

© 2014 Cengage Learning.

Pick Your Nose

Noses have a great deal of variation in structure, as shown in Figure 8.12. Once again, it pays to study classic nasal anatomy. You'll do a pastel sketch of one of these items from **Noses.jpg**. I pick the nose on the lower right.

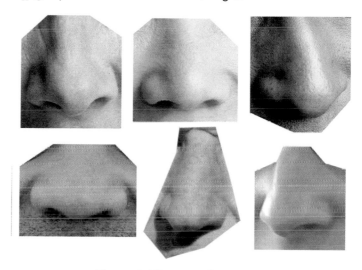

Figure 8.12 Contemplate your nasal.

© 2014 Cengage Learning.

Once again, work with tinted paper. Choose a somewhat more interesting texture than **Basic Paper**, such as **French Watercolor Paper**. Use the same custom palette and techniques that you used for the eye piece. This time the white highlights are more prominent, so get them down early. Figure 8.13 shows stages in rendering the nose.

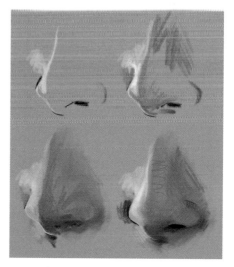

Figure 8.13 Nasal passages.

© 2014 Cengage Learning.

Have Another Sample

An alternative to using a Reference Image for sampling color is to simply have the photo open while you work. Hold down the **Option/Alt** key to access the **Dropper** tool. Click on the color you want, and release the modifier key. Your **Brush** tool returns.

Lip Service

The mouth is even more expressive than the eyes. There are variations in structure as well as in the relative sizes of upper and lower lips and their curvature. Figure 8.14 shows a few samples.

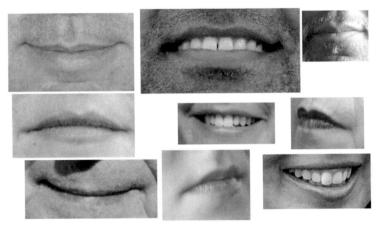

Figure 8.14 Oral majority.

© 2014 Cengage Learning.

Let's do a pastel drawing of Malik's mouth, in the center of the top row. As usual, begin with a rough sketch of the shapes and application of basic patches of color sampled form the photo. Smooth out some of the color with the **Blender**. Refine the shapes, and develop the tonal variations. In this case, one challenge is how to handle Malik's stubble. You can try to find an appropriate paper texture or make one yourself. I chose to use the **Scratchboard Rake** from the **Pens** category, at a reduced size with slight variablility in **Saturation** and **Value**. Figure 8.15 demonstrates the stages in the rendering of Malik's mouth on gray paper.

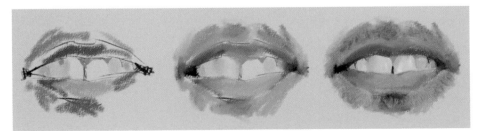

Figure 8.15 Malik's mouth.

© 2014 Cengage Learning.

Altogether Now

Using your newly acquired or sharpened skills, create a color rendering of the portrait of Stephen shown in Figure 8.16. That eye should look familiar!

Figure 8.16 Stephen.

© 2014 Cengage Learning.

Make a new image the same dimensions as the photo, with a pea-soup green paper color, similar to the background on the photo. You won't have **Tracing Paper** or **Cloner** brushes to rely on for accuracy, but there is a time-honored way to help you get the correct outlines and positions of the features: grid paper. **Window > Composition Panels > Layout Grid** opens the panel shown in Figure 8.17. Check the **Enable Layout Grid** box and set the **Vertical** and **Horizontal** divisions to 10. You may want to change the color of the grid lines for better contrast with the image. I used yellow.

Figure 8.17 Grid your lines.

Source: Corel ® Corporation.

With the layout grid enabled on both the photo and your blank canvas, carefully sketch Stephen's head in **Charcoal Pencil**, using a muted gray-green. Don't forget to include the shadow shapes under his nose and chin. My preliminary sketch is shown in Figure 8.18, alongside the gridded photo.

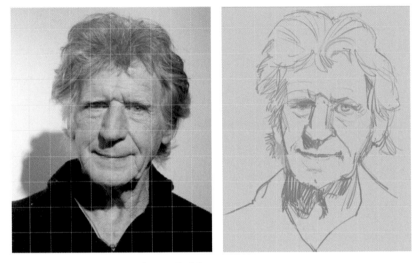

Figure 8.18 Stephen laid out.

© 2014 Cengage Learning.

Symmetry Is Overrated

Stephen is an excellent subject for a portrait because his face has the creases and bumps that come from maturity. This photo has strong directional lighting to provide contrast. One eye is almost completely in shadow, and the other eye makes a compelling focal point. When working on your own portrait subjects, try to avoid the common mistake of choosing smooth-faced children and beautiful young women. Subjects like Stephen are much more fun to draw!

If you like the drawing you did of Stephen's eye a few pages ago, why not copy and paste it into this portrait? It will give you a head start on the color rendering stage. You'll need to resize the eye to match the proportions of the portrait, as shown in Figure 8.19. If you don't like what you did before, here's your chance to get it right.

Open the photo of Stephen as a Reference Image so you can use the **Dropper** function for sampling colors. Notice the current **Paper** texture and change it to something bolder if needed. Use the **Soft Pastel** stick to lay in larger patches of color and the **Charcoal Pencil** for smaller areas. Sample color from the Reference Image frequently; there is a tremendous amout of color variation in the skin tones.

Dark Shadows

You don't need to follow sampled color slavishly. In particular, it's wise to avoid pure black in the shadows. Use dark browns, greens, and deep reds instead, for a much more realistic effect.

Figure 8.19 An eye for color.

© 2014 Cengage Learning.

Figure 8.20 shows the addition of color, with shadows rendered freely. Continue developing the facial structure, using a variety of directional strokes following the contours. Smooth a few areas with your **Smudge** blender, but leave other areas rough. Allow some bits of green paper to show through.

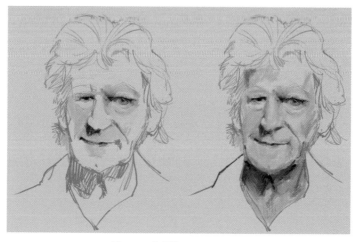

Figure 8.20 Adding color.

© 2014 Cengage Learning.

Looking at the "finished" portrait in Figure 8.21 with fresh eyes, I see that the eye I dropped in from my earlier drawing is too big. Recall that in accordance with typical proportions, the corner of the mouth lines up vertically with the center of the pupil. We'll have to fix that.

Figure 8.21 An eye for an eye.

Make a rectangular selection around the eye and use the **Transform** tool to reduce the size until the pupil lines up with the corner of Stephens' mouth. Be sure to disable the **Fast Preview** option so you can see the image selection instead of a gray box. The white space will have to be filled in with additional pastel drawing, as shown in Figure 8.22. This time around, I was able to capture some of the reticulated skin around Stephen's "new and improved" eye.

Figure 8.22 Eye surgery.

Composition

If you were creating this portrait using traditional oils, acrylic, or pastels, you could have corrected the eye without too much difficulty. What you could not do easily is add more paper or canvas to the portrait to improve the composition. Welcome to Painter's **Divine Proportion** feature, designed to help you establish the classically ideal areas to place focal points in your artwork. Use it before you begin painting, or use it now to fix the composition.

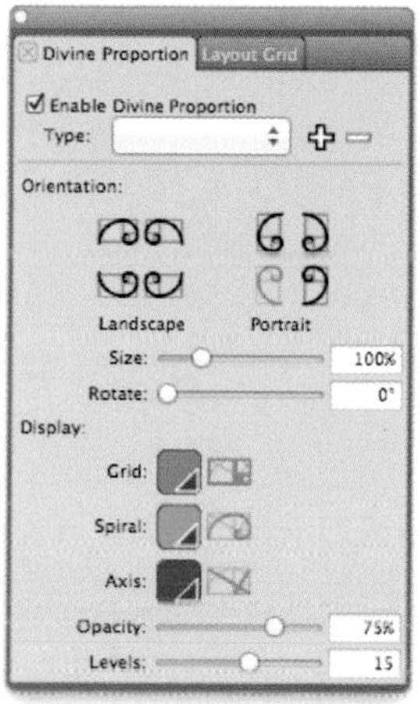

The **Divine Proportion** panel is grouped with the **Layout Grid** you used earlier. Enable it, and choose the portrait configuration, as shown in Figure 8.23.

Position the center of the spiral over Stephen's "dominant" eye, using the **Divine Proportion** tool. (It shares space with the **Perspective Guides** and **Layout Grid** in the **Toolbox**.) You can resize using the slider in the panel. With the **Divine Proportion** sized and positioned, it's clear you need to add quite a bit of canvas at the botton and some on the left of the drawing. Use **Canvas > Canvas Size** to add the pixels needed and fill them with the pea-soup color. Figure 8.24 shows the result. You now have some extra space for splashing in some additional pastel strokes to balance the head. The finished piece is shown in Figure 8.25.

Figure 8.23 How divine!

Source: Corel ® Corporation.

Figure 8.24 Compose yourself.

Source: Corel ® Corporation. Art © 2014 Cengage Learning.

Figure 8.25 Portrait of Stephen.

© 2014 Cengage Learning.

A Body of Work

In a typical figure drawing class, a nude model poses for increasing lengths of time, beginning with very short "gesture" poses lasting only a minute or two. Short poses can be very energetic and exciting to capture quickly with a few strokes. I often take my MacBook Pro and a Wacom tablet to figure drawing sessions. Figure 8.26 shows some 30-second to 2-minute live gesture drawings I created in Painter. The model changes position so quickly that there's no time to think—or blink! There's certainly no time to make corrections. But if you mess up, you've got a fresh start coming every minute or two.

Figure 8.26 Gesture poses.

Quick Study

Keeping up the fast pace of gesture drawing requires a stripped-down workspace to maximize efficiency and eliminate searching for tools, colors, and commands. This workspace, shown in Figure 8.27, is designed for the 15-inch screen of my MacBook Pro. It includes a custom palette with my favorite brush variants, a paper texture, and the very important **Iterative Save** command. The **Color Set** is limited to the flesh tints and bright accents I like. My **Layers** panel shows that a layer is in **Gel** mode, so that color will be transparent, allowing the ink lines on the canvas to show.

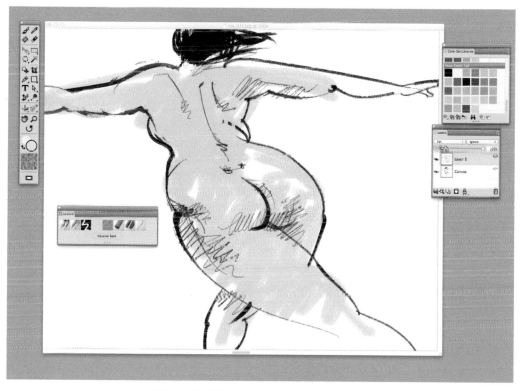

Figure 8.27 Gesture drawing workspace.

Source: Corel ® Corporation. Art © 2014 Cengage Learning.

Take a closer look at the custom palette, shown in Figure 8.28. There are three variants for drawing lines on the canvas. **Dry Ink** and the **Scratchboard Tool** are both **Pen** variants, so I made a custom icon for the **Scratchboard Tool**, to tell them apart at a glance. The **Real 6B Soft Pencil** is capable of responding to the tilt of my Wacom pen. The other items are useful for applying or blending color on the **Gel** layer.

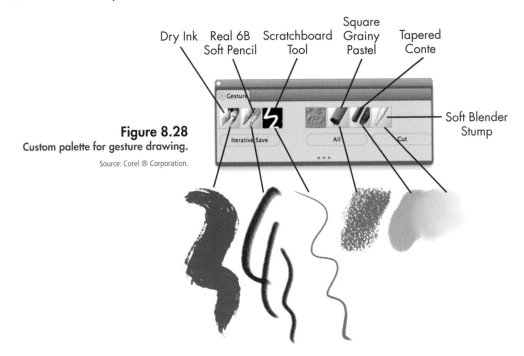

Figure 8.28
Custom palette for gesture drawing.

Source: Corel ® Corporation.

Make a **New Image** that fills most of your screen at 100% size, with enough room for the panels and palettes. **Open Rasa-warmup.jpg**, shown in Figure 8.29. Using any of the variants on the left side of the custom palette, make a few quick strokes on the canvas to express the pose. Save your sketch using the **Iterative Save** command and clear the canvas by pressing the [Select] **All** button followed by the [Edit] **Cut** button. Now repeat the process, using different variants or color. After each sketch, click the **Iterative Save** button and clear the canvas.

Figure 8.29
A graceful pose.

© 2014 Cengage Learning.

Your first few attempts might look like visual gibberish, but keep it up and you'll improve. Three of my efforts are shown in Figure 8.30. They were each done in about 30 seconds.

Figure 8.30 Don't erase; just do it again.

© 2014 Cengage Learning.

Naked Truth

Being forced to work this quickly encourages you to focus on the essence of the pose, skipping details. Just as important, this kind of practice helps you plunge into the process and ignore any self-doubts.

Ten Sketches in Ten Minutes

Open all ten of the images in the **Nudes** folder from the **Figure Drawing** folder. Stack them in any order you like; just be sure they don't cover up the blank canvas you'll be working on. If you can get someone to time you and holler "Next" every 60 seconds, you're good to go. Maybe there's a stopwatch app on your computer. Or set up a clock with a sweep second hand and keep one eye on it and your other eye on the photo. Don't worry about not having a third eye to look at your drawing—peripheral vision should be enough. In fact, the less you look at your drawing, the better. Ultimately, you may be able to produce a "blind gesture" sketch without looking at your drawing at all until it is done.

For each photo, make only the essential strokes to capture the essence of the pose. If there is time, add color on the **Gel** layer, but only to enhance the energy of the gesture. Use the same method for saving and clearing the canvas that you just practiced. Close each photo as soon as you finish it with the shortcut **Cmd/Ctrl+W**. You might want to add that command to your custom palette, using the **Custom Palette Organizer**.

What's Next?

In the next set of assignments, you'll continue exploring fine art techniques. Abstract painting will give you a break from reality, and you'll take the plunge into advanced Watercolor brushes.

9 fine Art Experiments

So far, you have had considerable practice drawing and painting what you see. Now you'll get a chance to create artwork that you don't see! This includes abstract painting as well as working with some of Painter's more esoteric features.

For this lesson, you'll use the following items from the website that supports this book:

- **Images:** Williams-Sonoma1.jpg, Williams-Sonoma2.jpg, purple_onions2.jpg

Don't Be Objective

There is a difference between abstract and nonobjective art. To oversimplify, "abstract" is reserved for artwork that is based in reality, whereas "nonobjective" is, well, not based on anything. It's just a collection of lines, shapes, tones, and textures. Actually, the essential elements for creating any kind of two-dimensional art are the same:

- **Line:** So many possibilities—straight or curved, smooth or jagged, bold or timid…

- **Shape:** Large or small, geometric or organic, simple or complex…

- **Tone (Color):** Dark or light, saturated or dull, warm or cool…

- **Texture:** Rough or smooth, subtle or strong, natural or synthetic…

Categories can overlap: a line that curves back on itself or is very fat becomes a shape. Lots of lines close together make a texture, and so on. The artist's job is to work out how to organize those elements on the canvas. A few basic principles, in no particular order, will help with that:

- **Contrast:** Not just brightness differences, but contrast in size, texture, or complexity of elements to create visual variety.

- **Repetition:** Create unity by repeating some of the elements, with variation in size, color, and angle.

- **Balance:** Composition, or placement of elements so that they work well within the picture plane.

- **Focal Point:** Create at least one center of interest, so it's not just "wallpaper."

Domestic Tranquility

Let's create an abstract still life based on a photo of high-end kitchen equipment. Open **Williams-Sonoma1.jpg**, shown in Figure 9.1. It is found in the **Domestic** section of the **Things** folder. You'll start by simplifying the shapes and obliterating details.

Use the **Smeary Varnish** variant from the **Impasto** category to create a painterly, messy version of the image, as shown in Figure 9.2. Because **Smeary Varnish** is an **Impasto** brush, there is depth and thickness to the bristly strokes. These will look best at 100% magnification. Use directional brush strokes that follow the forms to create visual variety while retaining just a hint of the original objects.

Figure 9.1   Kitchen window.

© 2014 Cengage Learning.

Figure 9.2   Messy kitchen.

© 2014 Cengage Learning.

Begin a new custom palette with the **Smeary Varnish** brush. Then add the items shown in Figure 9.3. Use the **Burn** and **Dodge** variants from the **Photo** category to darken or lighten pixels, respectively. The **Opaque Bristle Spray** brush is an **Impasto** variant that behaves like **Smeary Varnish**, but it also applies color.

Smeary Varnish   Real Stubby Blender

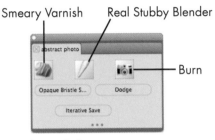

Burn

Figure 9.3 Abstract palette.

Source: Corel ® Corporation.

Following the principle that "less is more," choose an interesting rectangular area in your messy image and crop out everything else. My cropped version eliminates the right half of the image, as shown in Figure 9.4.

Figure 9.4 Crop the kitchen.

© 2014 Cengage Learning.

Recall that repetition is one of the principles for creating an effective painting. Use the **Rubber Stamp** tool, shown in Figure 9.5, to copy a few of the image elements to other locations in the painting. To establish the source area, hold the **Option/Alt** key when you click, and then release the modifier key and paint on the "destination" you want. Figure 9.6 shows a source and two destinations for repeating the element.

Figure 9.5 Rubber stamp.

Source: Corel ® Corporation.

Figure 9.6 Copy that!

© 2014 Cengage Learning.

Use **Smeary Varnish** to blend the edges of the repeated elements into the canvas and to create some variations. Figure 9.7 shows two other repetitions created with the **Rubber Stamp** technique. The irregular edge was created by using **Canvas > Canvas Size** to add blank pixels on each edge. Smears can then be made into the white border. The addition of yellow ochre strokes at the top and some dark gray on the left edge was done with the **Opaque Bristle Spray** brush, with color sampled from the painting.

Figure 9.7 Kitchen remodel.

© 2014 Cengage Learning.

Are We There Yet?

It can be difficult to tell when an abstract painting is done. If you've been using the **Iterative Save** command as you go, you can feel free to experiment with further changes, knowing you can always retrieve the previous version.

Rinse and Repeat

That painting was fun. Let's do something similar with the other Williams-Sonoma window display photo, shown in Figure 9.8.

Figure 9.8 More pots and pans.

© 2014 Cengage Learning.

Repeat the **Smeary Varnish** technique until you get results similar to what is shown in Figure 9.9.

Figure 9.9 Another fine mess.

© 2014 Cengage Learning.

Crop to a vertical selection that you want to develop. Continue simplifying with **Smeary Varnish** effects and use the **Opaque Bristle Spray** brush to add strokes using colors sampled from the image. Figure 9.10 shows this stage, with variable edges added.

Use the **Rubber Stamp** tool once again, or simply repeat some strokes freehand to create a better composition. If you need to add more tonal contrast, use the **Dodge** and **Burn** tools in your custom palette to lighten or darken some areas. Another kind of contrast involves texture. The painting is almost completely covered with striated impasto strokes. Some smooth, flat areas would help. Use the **Real Stubby Blender** to smooth out some spots. Figure 9.11 shows the final version. Consider printing your finished painting on canvas and then adding a few traditional oil or acrylic paint strokes for a truly mixed media piece. See the Appendix, "Fundamentals and Beyond," for other printing options and resources.

Figure 9.10 Smeared and cropped.

© 2014 Cengage Learning.

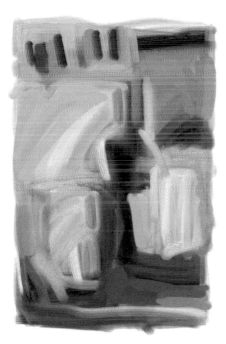

Figure 9.11 Modern kitchen.

© 2014 Cengage Learning.

Water Works

Way back in Lesson 5, "Painting People," you had an opportunity to work with Painter's **Digital Watercolor** brushes. Now you should be ready to tackle advanced watercolor brushes, which require their own special layer. Take some time getting to know the **Real Watercolor** category.

Figure 9.12 shows several of the variants, but what it doesn't show is how some of these brushes behave on their way to their final appearance. **Fractal Wash Wet**, for example, lightens up shortly after it is applied. **Melted Flow Map** creates realistic irregular mottling and "blooms" that can occur when paper has different degrees of wetness. Figure 9.13 shows stages in the development of a stroke made with the **Noisy Flow Map Fringe** variant. The longer your stroke, the more time needed for the process to be completed.

Play with the amazing **Real Watercolor** variants for a while. Explore different colors and paper textures. Try overlapping strokes. Notice that some variants fade or evolve over several seconds. Some develop a darker fringe on the edges.

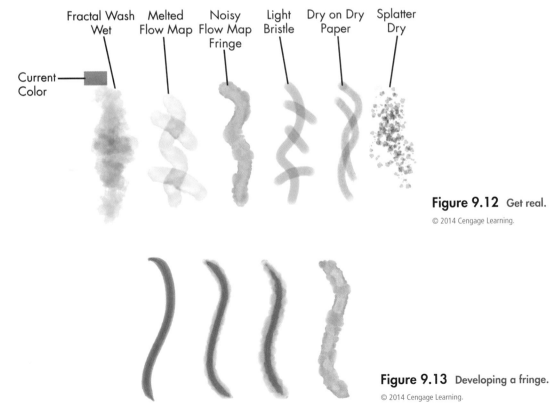

Figure 9.12 Get real.

© 2014 Cengage Learning.

Figure 9.13 Developing a fringe.

© 2014 Cengage Learning.

A Special Layer

When you apply a **Real Watercolor** stroke, Painter automatically creates a layer reserved only for these special variants. Not surprisingly, it is in **Gel** mode, for transparency. If you try to paint on a **Watercolor** layer with brushes from other categories, you get a warning (but not a ticket).

Make a custom palette, as shown in Figure 9.14. You may prefer different variants—there are 35 to choose from! Capture a custom icon for each variant from a test stroke, or use the **Show as Text** option.

Fractal Wash   Melted   Noisy Flow
Wet   Flow Map   Map Fringe

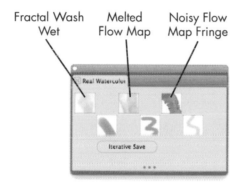

Figure 9.14 Real Watercolor strokes.

Source: Corel ® Corporation

Two of these variants use flow maps to determine how the stroke spreads as it diffuses into the paper. Like paper, patterns, and other media, flow maps are organized in a library, as shown in Figure 9.15. **Noisy Flow Map Fringe** shows a dramatic change resulting from your choice of flow map. The flow map effects in Figure 9.16 are, from left to right, Fine Dots, High Contrast Clouds, and Featherland.

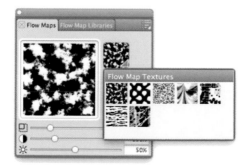

Figure 9.15 Go with the flow map.

Source: Corel ® Corporation.

Figure 9.16 Three noisy flow maps.

You can make your own flow map as easily as you can create a new paper texture. (See Lesson 4, "The Great Outdoors," to review that process.) Any selection in an image can be captured as a flow map element. I made the squiggles shown in Figure 9.17 with the **Dry Ink** brush and dragged a rectangular selection around them. Using the **Capture Flow Map** command in the **Flow Map** panel menu, I named it "Squiggles," and it become part of the current library, as shown in Figure 9.18.

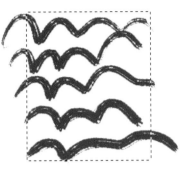

Figure 9.17 Ink squiggles.

© 2014 Cengage Learning.

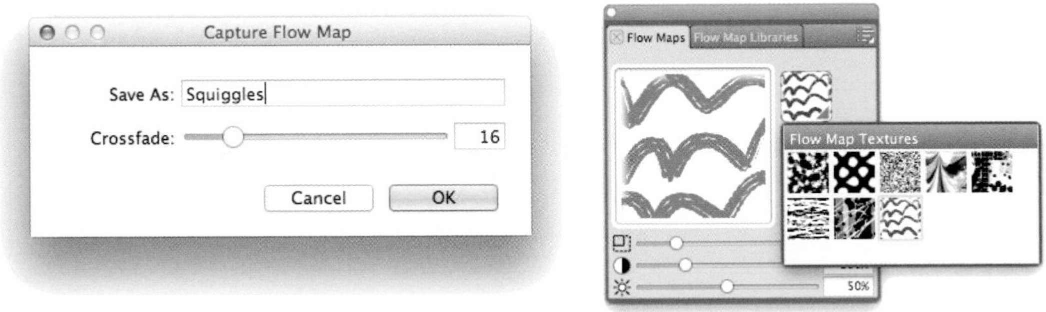

Figure 9.18 Capture and flow.

Source: Corel ® Corporation. Art © 2014 Cengage Learning.

Onions in Water

Open **purple_onions2.jpg**, a colorful array of produce shown in Figure 9.19. You'll use it to inspire a painting with **Real Watercolor** brushes.

Figure 9.19 Purple and green.

© 2014 Cengage Learning.

Open the photo as a Reference Image. Also, make a new **Color Set** from a selection similar to that shown in Figure 9.20. Choose **New Color Set from Selection** from the **Color Set** pop-up menu and specify 16 as the maximum number of colors. You can tweak the new **Color Set**, as needed. Using the icons at the bottom of the **Color Set** panel, you can delete any selected color swatch or add a swatch for your current color. There were too many nearly black colors in mine, so I deleted them. I also added pale yellow, a golden hue, and the teal blue sampled from the upper left of the photo. Figure 9.21 shows my adjusted **Color Set** for this project.

Figure 9.20 Set the colors.

© 2014 Cengage Learning.

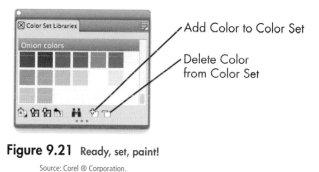

Add Color to Color Set

Delete Color from Color Set

Figure 9.21 Ready, set, paint!

Source: Corel ® Corporation.

Use **File > Quick Clone** to have access to **Tracing Paper**. Make a new layer and draw a rough sketch of the photo with a **Pencil** variant, similar to the one shown in Figure 9.22. This sketch layer will provide guidelines, but you will discard the sketch layer when the painting is finished.

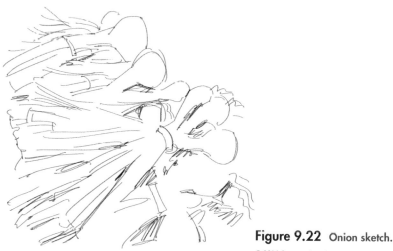

Figure 9.22 Onion sketch.

© 2014 Cengage Learning.

Begin applying watercolor strokes with the **Fractal Wash Wet** and **Noisy Flow Map Fringe** brushes. Choose **Gravel** for a simple flow map effect. Work from light to dark and start with larger forms before you get into details. Reduce the opacity of the sketch layer as your painting develops. Be sure to use the **Iterative Save** command to keep a record of stages as you work. Figures 9.23 and 9.24 show early stages in the painting.

Figure 9.23 Early onions.

© 2014 Cengage Learning.

Figure 9.24 Fractals and flow maps.

© 2014 Cengage Learning.

Grow Like an Onion

In the stage shown in Figure 9.25, visibility of the original sketch layer has been turned off. This version has richly layered color and some thinner lines made with **Real Wet Detail** strokes. Notice that this variant creates a stroke that is lighter in the center and has a darker wet fringe at the edges.

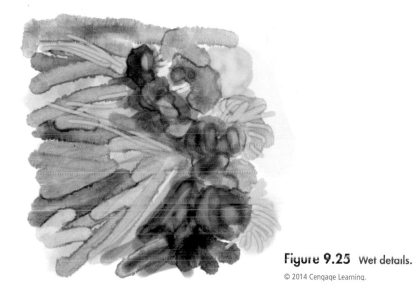

Figure 9.25 Wet details.

© 2014 Cengage Learning.

The detail in Figure 9.26 shows a method for lifting color, using wet-into-wet techniques. I wanted to produce some bright highlights on the onions. I discovered that using either **Light Bristle** or **Real Wet Detail** with the same reddish pink color would create the effect needed.

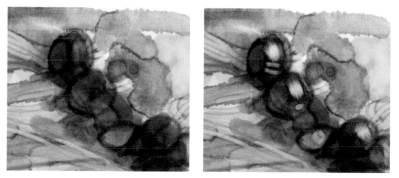

Figure 9.26 Wet into wet.

© 2014 Cengage Learning.

Take Back the Light

Traditional watercolorists have a number of tricks for removing pigment. If the paint is still wet, you can use a sponge or a paper towel to suck up the excess. Even after the paint is dry, you can try gentle scrubbing with a wet brush. Some of Painter's **Real Watercolor** variants naturally produce lighter areas when they finish "evolving."

If you have more patience than I do, your painting may be more realistic than mine, shown in Figure 9.27. I admit that my onions look more like radishes, but that's okay. The photo was just for jump-starting an experimental piece.

Figure 9.27 Onions, or radishes.

© 2014 Cengage Learning.

A Symmetry

Speaking of impatience, Painter offers a feature that can provide nearly instant gratification. **Mirror Painting** and **Kaleidoscope** effects will produce several strokes for every one you make. That's a labor-saving device any way you slice it. The **Kaleidoscope** feature provides as many as 12 such slices for complex repeats.

Choose the **Mirror Painting** tool and examine items in the **Property Bar**. The choices are slightly different depending on whether you switch to the **Kaleidosocope** option, shown in Figure 9.28.

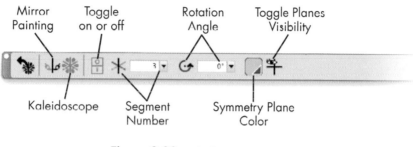

Figure 9.28 Kaleidoscope properties.

Source: Corel ® Corporation.

The simple design in Figure 9.29 was made with one turquoise stroke of a **Square Grainy Pastel** and two red strokes with the **Oil Pastel** variant. I used the default number of segments: three. For the next stage, I added to the number of segments. To avoid making a psychedelic snowflake, I moved the center, as shown In Figure 9.30. Switch from the **Brush** tool to the **Kaleidoscope** tool to change the center or angle of the segments. Be sure to choose the **Brush** tool again before you return to painting.

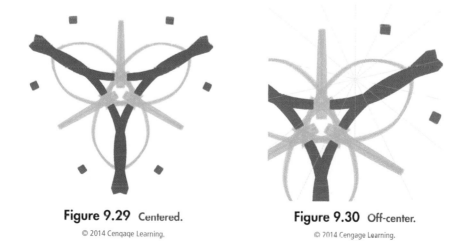

Figure 9.29 Centered.

© 2014 Cengage Learning.

Figure 9.30 Off-center.

© 2014 Cengage Learning.

Three yellow strokes created the sunburst in Figure 9.31. Another shift of center and a couple of marks with the **Felt Art Marker** complete the design.

Figure 9.31 Radiant radials.

© 2014 Cengage Learning.

The Other Kaleidoscope

Painter also has a kaleidoscope effect grouped with the **Dynamic** plug-ins, whose icon appears at the bottom of the **Layers** palette. This plug-in allows you to make a small square, creating kaleidoscopic effects that update as you move the square. Figure 9.32 shows where to find this effect.

Figure 9.32 Plug it in.

Source: Corel ® Corporation.

Practice using the **Dynamic Kaleidoscope** plug-in on some of the images from earlier in this lesson. When you choose the effect, you are prompted to enter a size in pixels. You can have as many dynamic kaleidoscope squares active in the image as you want. Figure 9.33 shows two 200-pixel kaleidoscope squares on my onions painting as well as one of the Williams-Sonoma abstract pieces.

Figure 9.33 Dynamic symmetry.

© 2014 Cengage Learning

When you're ready to commit to a design, use the **Convert to Default Layer** command in the **Layers** menu. You can stilll move the layer around, but it will not change. Of course, you can use any composite method you like.

What's Next?

Congratulations on making it through a lesson requiring you to stretch your skills and imagination. I invite you to come back and repeat some of these projects again with different source images or brush categories. Take your best paintings from this session and print them on canvas or watercolor paper specially made for desktop inkjet printers. If you want to produce large output, see the resource section in the Appendix.

In the next lesson, you'll continue to experiment with other exciting Painter features, and you'll meet our guest artist.

10 Special Projects

Would you like to give Painter more control over your artwork? Consider allowing it to take more responsibility for what you create. You'll do just that in this lesson. But first, meet the lovely and multitalented guest artist Claudia Salguero. She will show you how to create a lively urban illustration from start to finish. You'll hear her tell it in her own words, so you can enjoy her charming Colombian/Canadian accent.

For this lesson, you'll use the following items from the website that supports this book:

- **Images:** Naples.jpg, Paul.jpg

Claudia Salguero

Born in Bogota, Colombia, and based in Ottawa, Canada, Claudia is an award-winning photographer, graphic designer, fine artist, and Latin Jazz singer. Claudia blends photography and digital and traditional art into a magical mix of movement and color. She became a Corel Painter Master in 2007 and is the only artist from Latin America in this group.

Liquid City

To be honest, I was not interested in digital art until 2005. I was doing okay as a professional photographer and painting for myself. But life is full of surprises—and opportunities. The best thing that could have happened to me was a resolution problem with an image. I was able to solve my problem using Painter's cloning tools. This event changed my life as an artist!

Cityscapes are my favorite subject. I begin with photographs; then I use Painter to express the endless energy of interaction between people and places in the city.

Naples, Italy, is an intense, vibrant, and interesting city with amazing architecture. Its streets are full of life, people, motorcycles, cars, sounds, billboards, and balconies with colorful things hanging from them. I found Naples a fascinating place and couldn't help but create an image of it. Although sometimes I use several photos to create my paintings, in this case I used just one, shown in Figure 10.1.

All the information is there, and our job is to enhance the richness and life of the place. For that, let's use my favorite Painter tools and features:

- Distortion

- Liquid inks

- Layer composite methods

- Color adjustments

Figure 10.1 Naples, naturally.

© 2014 Cengage Learning.

Open **Naples.jpg**. The image has some dark areas to be illuminated and some lights and colors to be enriched. First, add some "air" around the image. To add white space around the edges, use **Canvas > Canvas Size** and enter **600** pixels in each dimension, as shown in Figure 10.2. Using 300 ppi (pixels per inch) makes the new image size about 8.5 × 11 inches, including the wide margins shown in Figure 10.3.

Figure 10.2 Add white pixels.

Source: Corel ® Corporation

Figure 10.3 Air space.

© 2014 Cengage Learning.

Put a copy of the photo on a new layer. Use **Select > All (Cmd/Ctrl+A)**, followed by **Edit > Copy (Cmd/Ctrl+C)** and **Edit > Paste (Cmd/Ctrl+V)**. Now the original image is on the canvas and a copy is on a layer. If you're planning to create an image with just some hints of color, you can convert this layer into black and white by lowering the color saturation to the minimum. Try using **Effects > Tonal Control > Adjust Color** with the setting shown in Figure 10.4.

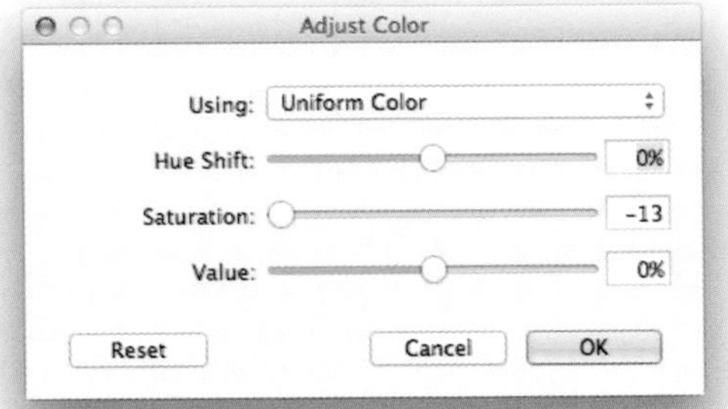

Figure 10.4 Eliminate color.

Source: Corel ® Corporation

Creative Distortion

You don't want the two men in the foreground right to be the focal point of the image. You can eliminate them by pulling pixels in on themselves to cover the areas you want to get rid of. Use the **Coarse Distorto** variant from the **F-X** category. The results are shown in Figure 10.5.

Figure 10.5 Two guys gone!

© 2014 Cengage Learning.

Coarse Distorto— A Versatile Tool

This variant from the **F-X** category is designed to move pixels around. Use it to distort, to apply color, and to eliminate some subjects.

You can use soft pastels to paint additional red poles and the missing part of the car. Then you can pull pixels around with **Coarse Distorto** as needed. This stage is shown in Figure 10.6.

Figure 10.6 Auto body work.

© 2014 Cengage Learning.

Use **Coarse Distorto** to pull some of the pixels at the edges of the grayscale image into the white margins, giving it even more movement and life. Figure 10.7 shows this stage. Then play with settings in the **Property Bar** to have longer or more grainy strokes.

Figure 10.7 Edge distortion.

© 2014 Cengage Learning.

Pixel Pulling

Distorto tools don't work in solid areas. They are designed to pull pixels around through different colors or tones. Raising the opacity of the **Coarse Distorto** brush can add color provided from the clone source or from the color wheel. Figure 10.8 shows the effect of zero opacity on the left and 90% opacity on the right.

Figure 10.8 From zero to 90.

© 2014 Cengage Learning.

Lively Liquids

Now the real fun starts! You can add some life to the balconies, enhancing them with **Liquid Inks**. Choose the **Coarse Bristle** variant and use the **Property Bar** settings shown in Figure 10.9: 50% opacity, 142% **Smoothness**, 40% **Volume**, and 1.4 **Feature**. Create two different **Liquid Ink** layers: one for white strokes and a second one for black strokes.

Figure 10.9 Liquid Ink settings.

Source: Corel ® Corporation.

Liquid Ink

A special layer is created automatically with your first **Liquid Ink** stroke. These variants don't work on default or watercolor layers. The reverse is also true: that is, you cannot use variants from other categories on a **Liquid Ink** layer. When you want to do so, you must convert the layer into a **Reference Layer**, using a command in the **Layers** menu. You can also create a new **Liquid Ink** layer with a command in the **Layers** menu.

I use **Liquid Ink** brushes because, at this point in my artistic growth, where I am in love with urban scenes (you never know what is next!), they are my favorite brush category to give expression to my subjects. **Liquid Ink** brushes are versatile, fast, accurate, and clean. The strokes look handmade, graffiti-like, young, and energetic—definitely urban.

Figure 10.10 shows the effect created with lively **Liquid Ink** strokes on the balconies, around the signs, and in other spots. Take a close look at the balconies' lines in the detail shown in Figure 10.11. Notice that some strokes are black, some are white, and others are gray. This effect is created by changing the black **Liquid Ink** layer to the **Reverse-Out** method. Try all the composite method options—results can be not only useful but spectacular!

Figure 10.10 Bristly balconies.

© 2014 Cengage Learning.

Figure 10.11 Composite method magic.

© 2014 Cengage Learning.

Finishing Touches

There is definitely something missing—color. Recall that the original full-color image is underneath the layers. Simply erasing parts of the grayscale layer reveals colored areas on the canvas. Figure 10.12 shows how the grayscale layer might look after significant erasing.

Figure 10.12 Erasable Naples.

As the final touch, add some shades and lights to the **Liquid Ink** lines, giving the balconies and buildings more volume and expression. A close-up detail is shown in Figure 10.13, and the finished artwork appears in Figure 10.14.

Figure 10.13 Neopolitan detail.

© 2014 Cengage Learning.

Figure 10.14 Viva Napoli!

© 2014 Cengage Learning.

Automated Portraiture

I generally prefer to apply my own brushstrokes one at a time, but I'll make an exception for the amazing **Auto-Painting** feature. This allows Painter to create a cloned painting based on the brush variants chosen, and a few other parameters. Figure 10.15 shows stages in an image I created for the previous edition of this book. It is among the examples of artwork provided in the Welcome screen when you launch Painter X3. Here's a chance to do something similar with a photo of Paul.

Figure 10.15 Martin in stages.

© 2014 Cengage Learning.

Open **Paul.jpg** from the **People > Heads** folder. Enhance the photo's color by choosing the **Impressionist Color Scheme** in the **Underpainting** panel. Figure 10.16 shows the new color scheme.

Figure 10.16 Impressionist Paul.

© 2014 Cengage Learning.

Get Smart

Open the **Auto-Painting** panel and check both the **Smart Stroke Painting** and **Smart Settings** boxes, as shown in Figure 10.17. **Smart Settings** automatically adjust the size, length, and pressure of strokes based on the amount of detail in the photo. With both of those features enabled, none of the other options are available, except the speed slider.

The enhanced photo of Paul should make a good (and fast) impressionist painting. Use **File > Clone** and choose the **Impressionist** brush from the **Artists** category. Click the **Rubber Stamp** icon on the color wheel panel to enable clone color, and press the **Play** button on the **Auto-Painting** panel. When you are satisfied with the result, click the **Stop** button. Your result should look something like the image in Figure 10.18. Notice that brush strokes follow the contours of Paul's face. Those really are Smart Strokes!

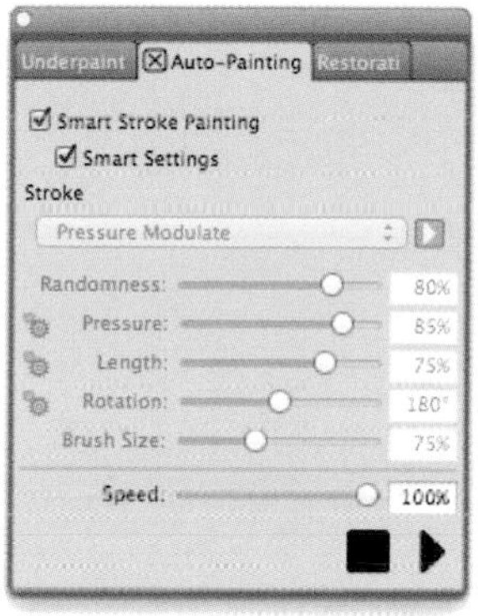

Figure 10.17 Smart boxes checked.

Source: Corel ® Corporation.

Figure 10.18 An impressionable young man.

© 2014 Cengage Learning.

That was just a warm-up for some deeper exploration of Auto-Painting. Make a custom palette for the next stage, using the items shown in Figure 10.19 as suggestions. Feel free to add or substitute some of your favorite variants.

That Smarts!

One of the variants in this custom palette is **Acrylic Captured Bristle** from the **Smart Stroke** category, supposedly optimized for Auto-Painting. There is a "regular" **Captured Bristle** in the **Acrylic** category. If you can find any difference in their behavior, you're smarter than I am.

Smart Strokes: Acrylic Captured Bristle   Artists: Sargent Super Jitter

Artists: Impressionist

Acrylics: Grainy Dry Brush

Artists: Van Gogh

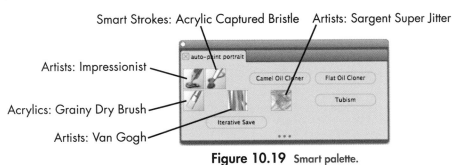

Figure 10.19 Smart palette.

Source: Corel ® Corporation. Art © 2014 Cengage Learning.

Semi-Automatic

Uncheck **Smart Stroke Painting**. You now have access to a long list of stroke styles, including **Swirly**, **Squiggle**, and **Splat**. Figure 10.20 shows **Zig Zag** as the current stroke. Imagine how much fun you're about to have trying out combinations of brush variants and stroke styles! Choose either a **Cloner** variant or any other brush with **Clone Color** enabled.

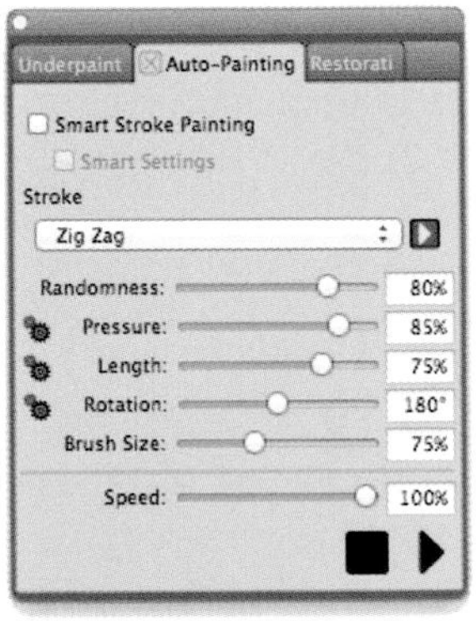

Figure 10.20 Have a stroke.

Source: Corel ® Corporation

To produce something similar to Figure 10.21, use **Sargent Super Jitter** with the **Zig Zag** stroke. Click the **Play** button at the bottom right of the panel, and watch what happens. When you like what you see, click the **Stop** button.

Figure 10.21 Super Jitter Zig Zag.

© 2014 Cengage Learning.

Intelligent Designs

Clearly, you have considerable influence over the development of an automated painting. You can make your mark by choosing brushes, creating layered composites, and using a variety of stroke styles available when you disable **Smart Stroke Painting**.

The **Sargent Super Jitter** results work well as an underpainting, but much bolder color effects are needed. Explore other variants until you get something you want to keep, and remember to use **Iterative Save** as you develop the painting. You can undo any Play-Stop sequence that doesn't please you. Figure 10.22 shows what happens when you switch to the **Grainy Dry Brush** (an Acrylic variant) along with the **Squiggle** stroke.

This brush has a wonderful ability to pick up more than one color in a stroke, so it's desirable to experiment with some other stroke styles. Swirly is used for the stage shown in Figure 10.23.

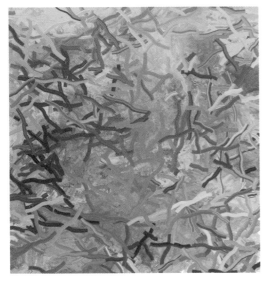

Figure 10.22 Acrylic Dry Squiggle.

© 2014 Cengage Learning.

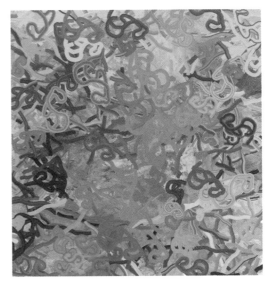

Figure 10.23 Dry Swirly.

© 2014 Cengage Learning.

At this point, the challenge is to make Paul's face more recognizable, while allowing the rest of the image to be wild and abstract. Smaller size strokes reveal more detail, and you can restrict those effects to the face by using an oval selection, as shown in Figure 10.24. Then apply the **Medium Dab** stroke.

Figure 10.24 Face Dabs.

© 2014 Cengage Learning.

Make smaller oval selections on the mouth and eye areas, and switch to the **Short Dab** stroke. Finally, make a lasso selection around the sideburn and jaw and apply the **Single Sketch Line** stroke. The final version (if it really is final) is shown in Figure 10.25.

Figure 10.25 Paul's smart portrait.

© 2014 Cengage Learning.

What's Next?

That's totally up to you! Go back and revisit some of the projects, using different source images or techniques. Explore some of Painter's features I didn't get around to showing you. Use Painter in your professional work or for personal fulfillment. But, above all, have fun with it.

A fundamentals and Beyond

In these few pages, you'll find some recommendations useful for continuing with digital painting after you're finished with this book. But first, there are a few things to discuss that will get you off on the right foot, if it's not too late.

Pixels Versus Vectors

Painter and Photoshop are pixel based. The word *pixel* is short for picture element, using the common abbreviation *pix* for *picture*. Each pixel represents a tiny colored dot or square, and with enough of them lined up horizontally and vertically, you'll get the picture. Resolution, measured in pixels per inch or ppi, tells you about the quality of the image. A resolution of 300 ppi has a much finer grain and more detail than the same image at 72 ppi. Resolution is especially important when images are prepared for printing. Pixel-based (aka raster or bitmap) images must include information on the color and location of every one of those pixels. Depending on the dimensions and resolution, there can be thousands of such pixels in an image, resulting in hefty file sizes. For example, a Painter or Photoshop file that's 8" × 10" at 300 ppi weighs in at 20MB. The larger the file size, the more RAM that is needed and the harder your computer has to work.

By contrast, vector-based programs like Flash and Illustrator are resolution independent and have the advantage of smaller files, because the image elements this time are not pixels but paths with simple fills and strokes (outlines) that can be stored as mathematical instructions. By their nature, vector-based images tend to have hard-edged lines and flat color fills, whereas pixel-based graphics can have the kind of variation called *continuous tone*, seen in photos and traditional paintings. Working with pixels is intuitive and natural, in my opinion, but it takes considerable practice to become skilled at placing the anchor points and adjusting the curves that make up vector shapes.

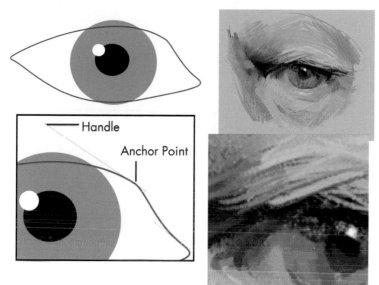

Figure A.1 Vectors vs. pixels.

© 2014 Cengage Learning.

These eyes show you the difference between pixels and vectors rather dramatically. The eye on the right was created in a project from Chapter 8, "Life Drawing." The zoomed-in detail lets you see some pixels up close and personal. The eye on the left shows my lame attempt to work with vector shapes. It has hard edges. The close-up shows a couple of anchor points and the handles required for adjusting curve segments. There are pros and cons to each approach, and you don't have to restrict yourself to just one or the other. If you're not sure which category you prefer, ask yourself if you'd rather have precision or instant gratification. Do you like being able to create clean, sharp lines or juicy, smeary ones? I knew I was a pixel-packin' mama from the start!

The Best of Both Worlds

Pixel pushers can have access to some of the benefits of the vector world. Using **File > Acquire**, you can open Adobe Illustrator files that are in .ai or .eps (encapsulated postscript) format and see each shape in your **Layers** palette. When you save your image, you must convert these vector elements to pixels (or *rasterize* them, which sounds much more exotic).

Save As

I just mentioned two file formats used by vector images: .ai (Adobe Illustrator) and .eps. Here's a list of the most basic file formats Painter uses and other pixel-based applications, along with hints on how to choose the best one for your purpose:

- **RIFF (Raster Image File Format):** This is Painter's native format. Images you create in Painter are automatically saved as RIFF files. You need this file format to preserve elements unique to Painter, such as **Dynamic**, **Watercolor**, or **Liquid Ink** layers. RIFF is also necessary for the **Iterative Save** function. Other applications do not recognize RIFF files.

- **PSD (Photoshop Document):** If your Painter image has default layers (not specialized layers, such as **Dynamic**, **Watercolor**, or **Liquid Ink**), and you want to switch easily between Painter and Photoshop, use the PSD format. Painter's masks will be preserved as Photoshop channels. However, not all of Painter's composite methods have equivalents to Photoshop blending modes, and text layers will not survive the transition.

- **TIFF (Tagged Image File Format):** This popular format does not preserve layers, dropping them all into the background. You can save a mask if you use the **Save Alpha** check box. (*Alpha* is Photoshop's term for additional channels created from saved selection masks.)

- **JPEG (Joint Photographic Experts Group):** A handy format for compressing an image file to make it load quickly on a website or transmit quickly as an email attachment. This compression is *lossy*, meaning the quality of an image suffers if it is compressed over and over or if you use low-quality settings. Be sure to save a copy of your image in another format that will keep its quality intact.

- **GIF (Graphics Interchange Format):** This is the option specifically designed for most nonphotographic images used on the web. Colors are reduced to 256 or fewer, and you have several choices for minimizing file size. It's an ideal format for small animated images on the web.

- **PNG (Portable Network Graphics):** Using a lossless compression method, this format is superior to GIF for transferring images on the Internet. For one thing, PNG allows portions of an image to be transparent. Painter 11 was the first version to be PNG-able.

- **TARGA (Truevision Advanced Raster Graphics Adapter):** This was the native format of the first graphics cards for IBM-compatible PCs to support high-end color display. The compression method used in Targa images performs poorly when compressing images with many color variations, such as digital photos, but it works well for simpler images.

- **BMP (BitMaP):** On the Microsoft Windows operating system (OS), this is a Raster graphics image file format used to store pixel-based images independently of the display device.

- **PCX (Personal Computer eXchange):** The native file format for PC Paintbrush, developed by the now-defunct ZSoft Corporation. It has been succeeded by more sophisticated image formats, such as GIF, JPEG, and PNG.

Running the Gamuts

Advanced color theory and prepress technology are beyond the scope of this book, but a few basic color concepts can help you manage. Here are the color terms used in this book, and a few more for good measure.

- **HSV (Hue, Saturation, Value):** *Hue* is a position on the spectrum. The words *red, orange,* and *green* refer to hues but are very inexact. You need to know how pure the color is (*Saturation*) and how bright or dark it is (*Value*). Other terms for *value* are *brightness, lightness,* and *luminosity,* all of which are used in Painter in various contexts. The right portion of Figure A.2 shows HSV values displayed as numerical settings for a specific blue in the **Color** palette.

- **RGB (Red, Green, Blue):** The RGB color model is additive, involving colors emitted from a light source. This color space is useful for describing colors on your monitor. The left portion of Figure A.2 shows the current color with its **Red**, **Green**, and **Blue** components indicated.

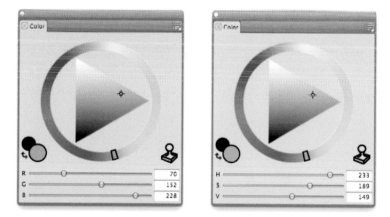

Figure A.2 RGB and HSV.

Source: Corel ® Corporation.

- **CMYK (Cyan, Magenta, Yellow, blacK):** This color space is subtractive, involving reflected color from a mixture of paints, dyes, or inks. Painter does not use the CMYK color space. You need to use another program, like Photoshop, to convert your artwork to CMYK mode for commercial printing.

- **Gamut:** Gamut is the entire range of colors that is available in a given color space. RGB has a larger gamut than CMYK, especially for highly saturated colors. This explains why some colors that look great on your monitor don't look so good in print.

Painter provides a color management feature, available in the **Canvas** menu. The settings, shown in Figure A.3, include a number of options for assigning and converting to color profiles. Your choices depend on your purpose, such as the kind of printing you plan to do. You might need to ask an expert for advice.

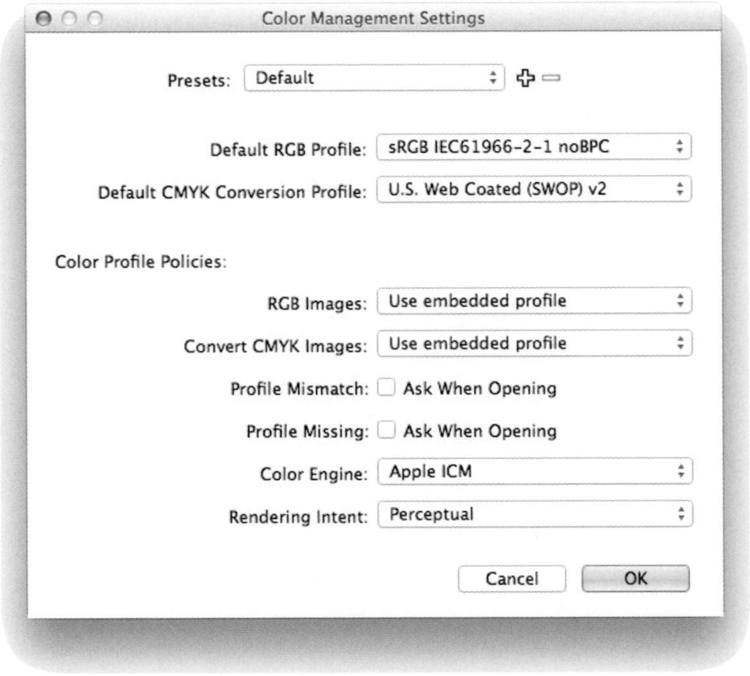

Figure A.3 Color Manager.

Source: Corel ® Corporation.

Pick a Tablet

Wacom makes a range of tablets in several sizes, for every budget and work situation, starting with the entry-level Bamboo series and maxing out at the Cintiq, which is actually a monitor you can draw on. My personal choice is the mid-range Intuos series, and my preferred size is the very portable 6" × 9".

The Wacom website, www.wacom.com, is as user friendly as can be, offering you help in deciding which tablet is best for you, downloads for updating drivers, and technical support. It even hosts a community of photographers, illustrators, designers, and mixed media artists for discussions, competitions, and posting of images. Check out the Wacom Facebook page.

Your tablet should automatically be in "pen mode" after you install the driver software, so every point on the tablet has a matching point on the screen. When you move your pen over the tablet, the cursor moves in precisely the same way on the screen. Where you touch your pen tip to the tablet is a click. If you need to customize the mapping relationship, use the Wacom Tablet preferences. The section for mapping is shown in Figure A.4. This is the Mac version, found in **System Preferences**. The way to find this control panel on a PC is as follows: click on **Start > All Programs > Wacom Tablet > Wacom Tablet Properties**. The default configuration is full screen mapped to full tablet, but you can designate only a portion of the screen (or tablet) for point-to-point matching.

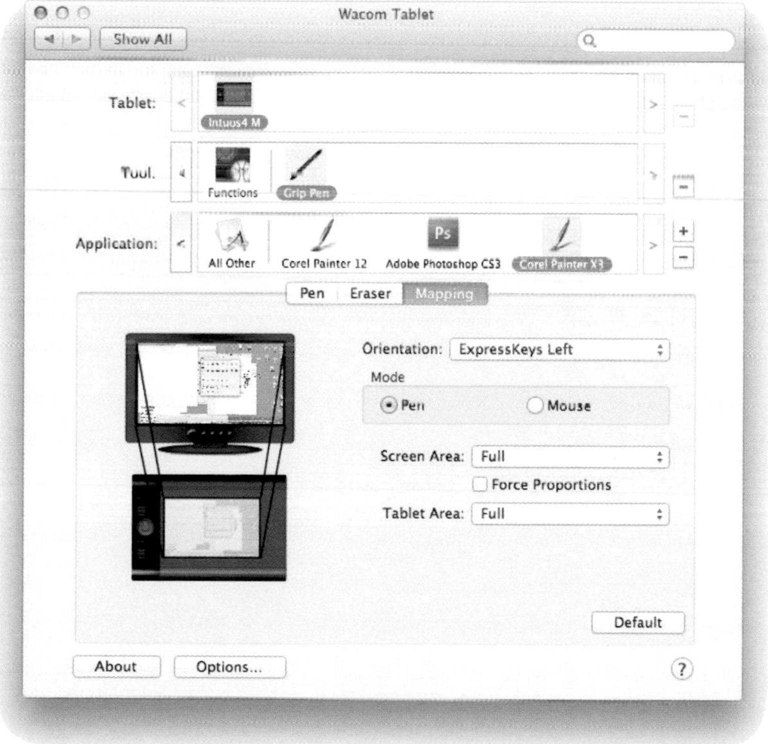

Figure A.4 Tablet mapping.

Source: Wacom.

Figure A.5 shows the Wacom control panel with options for the Pen selected. The lever on the pen barrel has two positions that are capable of double-click and right-click actions by default, but each can be programmed for a variety of other purposes. I routinely disable the lever, because I don't want to be annoyed by accidental clicks or popup menus as I paint. The Intuos tablet itself has several customizable buttons that will make numerous trips to the keyboard unnecessary.

Notice the upper section of the panel, where you can specify which tablet or stylus you are using. You can add applications and create custom settings for each of them.

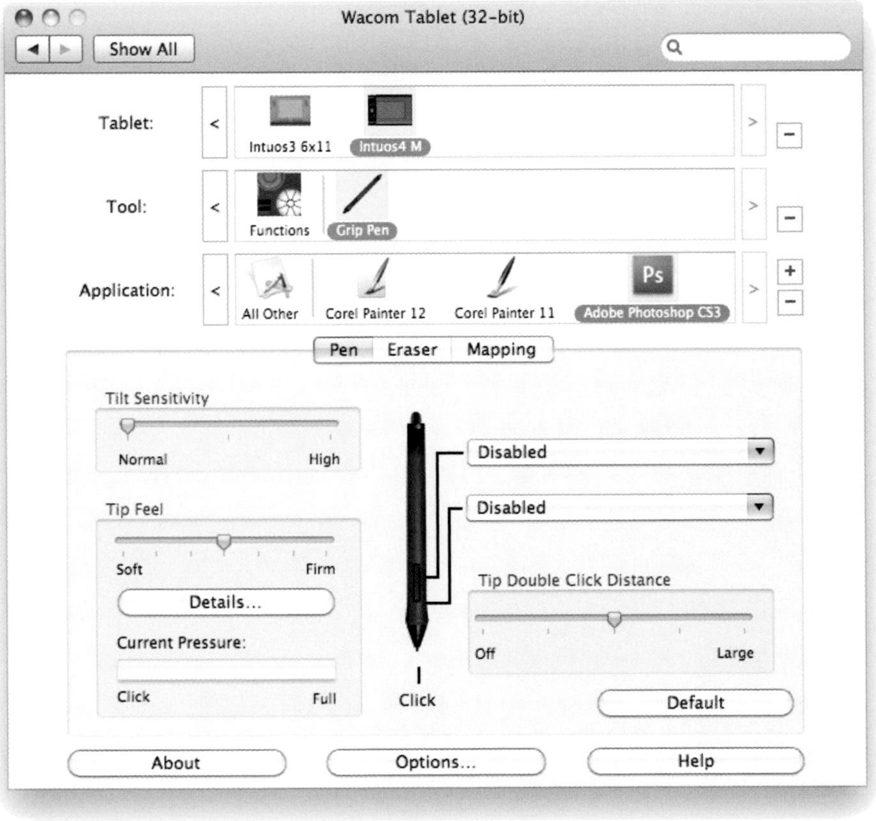

Figure A.5 Pen pointers.

Source: Wacom.

Some of the many customizing options for the Intuos tablet are shown in Figure A.6. When you click the **Functions** icon in the **Tool** field, options for programming tablet buttons are available. This view shows the default functions for the **ExpressKeys**, along with menus that allow other choices for each button. Additional displays for the **TouchRing** and **Radial Menu** button are not shown. An Intuos tablet offers a variety of special options and features. I suggest you get accustomed to using the default functions for each **ExpressKey**. The **TouchRing** is a handy way to zoom in and out and to change brush sizes on the fly.

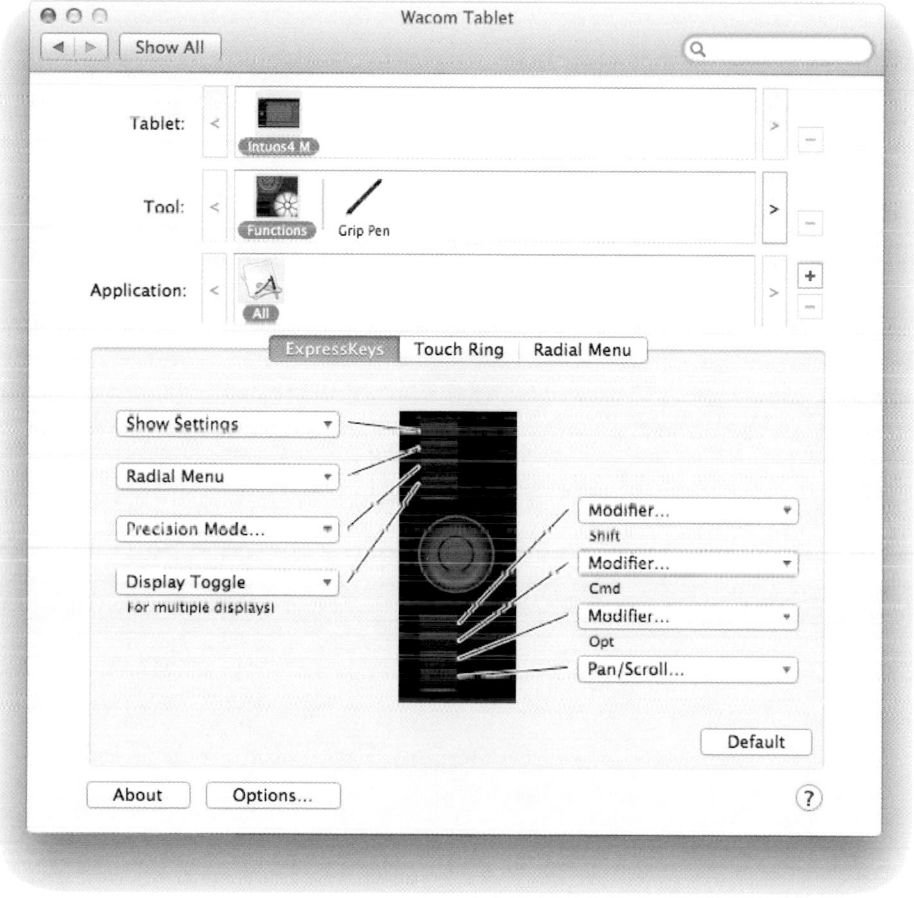

Figure A.6 Don't forget your Keys.

Source: Wacom.

Use a Shortcut

Another excellent way to increase speed and efficiency (if you're into that sort of thing) is to learn the keyboard shortcuts for the most frequently used commands. Use Table A.1 as a reference. Some of these are specific to Painter, but most are used by all programs, so you might know them already. A couple of modifier keys are different for Mac versus PC users. On the Windows platform, the **Ctrl** key corresponds to the **Command** key on a Mac. (That's the key with the Apple logo, or the thing that looks like a four-leaf clover with an eating disorder.) The **Alt** key on a PC is the equivalent of the **Option** key for Mac users. There are a few other differences, like **Delete** serving the same purpose as **Backspace**.

Table A.1   Keyboard Shortcuts

Menu Command	Mac	PC
File > New	Cmd+N	Ctrl+N
File > Open	Cmd+O	Ctrl+O
File > Save	Cmd+S	Ctrl+S
File > Save As	Shift+Cmd+S	Shift+Ctrl+S
File > Iterative Save	Option+Cmd+S	Alt+Ctrl+S
File > Close	Cmd+W	Ctrl+W
File > Print	Cmd+P	Ctrl+P
Edit > Undo	Cmd+Z	Ctrl+Z
Edit > Redo	Cmd+Y	Ctrl+Y
Edit > Copy	Cmd+C	Ctrl+C
Edit > Paste	Cmd+V	Ctrl+V
Select > All	Cmd+A	Ctrl+A
Select > None (Deselect)	Cmd+D	Ctrl+D
Select > Hide/Show Marquee	Shift+Cmd+H	Shift+Ctrl+H
Window > Zoom In	Cmd+ + (plus sign)	Ctrl+ + (plus sign)
Window > Zoom Out	Cmd+ − (minus sign)	Ctrl+ − (minus sign)
Window > Zoom to Fit	Cmd+0 (zero)	Ctrl+0 (zero)
Window > Screen Mode Toggle	Cmd+M	Ctrl+M

Get Off My Intellectual Property!

Here's some free legal advice, and I assure you it's worth every penny.

If you scan images printed in books or magazines or search the web for digital pictures, be aware that such items might be copyright protected. That's not a problem unless you want to publish your edited versions. Copyright law gives the original creator of an image all rights to it, including derivations thereof. (Or is it "wherefrom?") How much would you have to change an image to make it legally your own and not just a derivation? Are you willing to go to court to find out?

When it comes to using the likeness of a celebrity, things can get complicated. Are you infringing on the copyright of the subject or the photographer who created the photo? Maybe both. Famous people have the *right of publicity* to prevent others from making money with their likeness, even after death. On the other hand, ordinary folks have the right to privacy, so you need to get a "model release" signed before you can legally publish their faces.

There are exceptions to copyright protection, called *fair use*. For example, you can publish doctored images of famous people for satirical purposes. Copyright expires 70 years after the death of the creator (last time I checked), after which the image becomes *public domain*, so anything goes. An image like the *Mona Lisa* is *way* in the public domain, even though the actual painting is owned by the Louvre in Paris. Ownership of a piece of art is completely separate from usage rights thereto. The images made available to you on the website that supports this book are provided only for your personal use in working the projects. All other rights are reserved by the copyright holders.

Resources

This section suggests sources for more training, images to play with, media to print on, and even places to display your work to other digital painters.

There is instant access to online tutorials and the Painter community from your **Help** menu. Choose **Help > Tutorials** and click on **Painter**. This takes you to a page where you can select from a variety of video tutorials, webinars, and other training options. You can look at the work of dozens of Painter Masters, including John Derry, one of the original creators of the program. Jeremy Sutton has a set of Painter X3 tutorial videos on PaintboxTV.com, which I recommend as a complement to this book. You'll enjoy learning his creative approaches, delivered in a charming British accent. And if you can handle a barely annoying Chicago accent, check out my Painter X3 DVD training from InfiniteSkills.com.

When you launch Painter, don't be too quick to dismiss the welcome screen, shown in Figure A.7. The menu on the left not only provides quick access to your own images and workspaces, but is another point for entry into online resources for Painter.

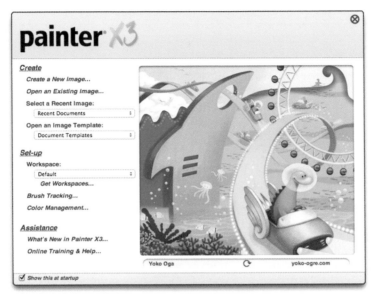

Figure A.7 You're welcome.

Source: Corel ® Corporation.

Finding Images

You'll probably want to shoot most of your own source photos, but when you need a variety of images or something unusual in a hurry, use the Internet. If you don't mind low resolution and are careful about possible copyright issues, use Google's search engine. When you get to the Google home page at www.google.com, click on **Images** instead of **Web** and type in what you're looking for. This is a great way to get visual references for accuracy or just browse for ideas.

There are commercial online sources for high-quality stock photography. They generally require payment of fees for specified usage, and their target market is professional designers and illustrators. If you want a lot of images, those fees can really add up. For stock images with a liberal licensing agreement at bargain prices, my vote goes to Shutterstock.com. It's easy to use Shutterstock's Boolean search engine to find what you need quickly and, best of all, you can subscribe for a relatively small fee, considering the volume of images you'll get.

One month of this service costs $249 the last time I checked and allows you 25 images per day or a total of 750 photos for the month. That's about 33 cents per image. Other companies can charge $200 for a single photo! Check it out: www.shutterstock.com.

Consider using your older (analog) photos. Take old snapshots out of the family album or the shoebox and digitize them. A basic scanner is pretty cheap and is a handy device to have around. If you want to digitize images found in books or magazines, your scanner should have a Descreen feature. This is needed to prevent an unsightly *moiré pattern* from the halftone dots used in process printing. Published images are almost certainly copyright protected; that's not a problem if you're just using them in the privacy of your own home and with consenting adults.

Color Printing

A good inkjet printer can provide excellent output as long as you use high-quality paper or other media to print on. Ordinary paper is too porous, letting ink spread into the fibers, so images get blurry or muddy looking. Given the gamut limitations that come with the territory, my choice for crisp rich color is glossy photo paper. Epson and HP make it, among others. It comes in various weights and can be glossy on both sides.

For wearable art, consider printing your images on iron-on transfers that can be applied to clothing, hats, or what-have-you. Avery makes inkjet magnet sheets, which I print with several small images. Then I trim them into shapes for some unique refrigerator magnets.

Archival-quality papers are available for fine art printing from your desktop. A great resource is Digital Art Supplies (www.digitalartsupplies.com), where you can find a range of high-end papers, fabric, and canvas. If you plan to print on canvas, you won't need to add an optical canvas texture to your artwork. This company offers several beautiful Japanese papers that I use for printing my nude gesture drawings.

If you want to print big but don't want to invest in a large-format printer, order from an outfit like www.imagers.com/poster.html. Visit the website for a price list of poster sizes from 18"×24" to 59"×96" printed on photo paper, film, vinyl, or canvas.

Fonts

After using the **Text** tool for a while, you might get a hankering for more exciting typefaces than just the ones that are factory-installed on your computer. Lots of fonts are available free, or nearly free, for personal and commercial use. You can download them from sites like Typodermic Fonts (formerly known as Larabie fonts): www.10000fonts.com/index.htm?hop=typodermic.

That's where you'll find the aptly named Ultimate Font Download—10,000 fonts for only $29.99. Such a deal!

If you need a special font and are willing to pay a little more for it, there are quite a few possibilities. LetterHead Fonts specializes in rare and unique fonts for artists and designers. The home page is breathtaking, and browsing this site is pure pleasure: www.letterheadfonts.com. Fonthead Design, http://fonthead.com, sells distinctive and whimsical display fonts starting at $15 each. Several collections of about a dozen fonts grouped by themes, such as Old Writing or Rough and Tough, are sold for $39 per volume. Fonthead makes, GoodDog and CatScratch, two of my personal favorites. GoodDog, shown in Figure A.8, is actually a free-bee, as is a set of cartoon face dingbats (small decorative images or symbols) called Font Heads. CatScratch can be found in the Rough and Tough collection.

Consider having your own handwriting converted into a font. There's a free online tool for that, available at www.myscriptfont.com.

ABCDEFGHIJKLM
NOPQRSTUVWXYZ
abcdefghijklm
nopqrstuvwxyz
0123456789!?#
%&$@*{(/|\)}

Figure A.8 Who's a good dog?

Source: fonthead.com.

Gallery

At the Beach. Digital watercolor painting based on a photo.

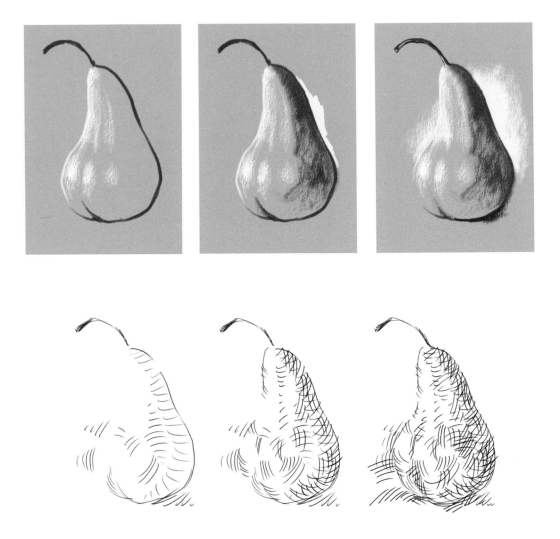

Developing a Pear. Two techniques for drawing a pear. Top shows stages in drawing on tinted paper with Conte and Hard Pastel variants. Bottom shows cross-hatching the contours of the fruit with the 2B Pencil.

Live Caricatures. Examples of my digital caricatures created live at conventions, trade shows, and corporate events, spanning nearly 20 years.

Double Portrait. I combined two separate photos to make this cloned portrait of a couple.

Drawing a Pepper. Two techniques for cloning a chili pepper from a photo.
On the left: Grainy Colored Pencil. On the right: Tapered Pastel., Pointed Stump (Blender), and Sharp Chalk.

© 2014 Cengage Learning.

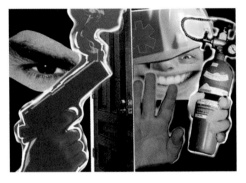

Editorial Illustration. Commissioned for the trade magazine *Emergency Medical Services.*
The article was titled "Create the Carnage and We Will Come," and it was about the tendency for rescue
workers to plunge into dangerous situations without sufficient regard for their own safety.

Hawaiian Heliconia. A painting using Digital Watercolor variants.

Digital Doodles. Just fooling around, mostly with the Scratchboard Tool from the Pens category and Paint Bucket fills. The doodle on the lower left was made with Dry Ink and Oil Pastel followed by smudging with a Blender variant.

© 2014 Cengage Learning.

Man and Dog. Remember David Letterman? Well, none of these facial features are his! I borrowed the mouth from Elton John and the eyes, nose, and hands from other celebrity photos. That's not really the dog's mouth, either.

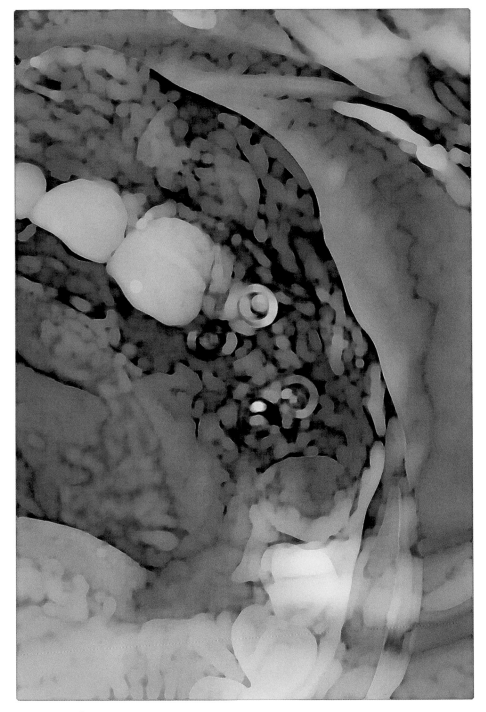

Mouthscape. This painting began with a photo of the inside of my mouth, during a procedure to install implants. A printed version hangs in my dentist's office.

Painter X (Ten) Self-Portrait. Based on a photo of me working as a digital caricature artist at an event. I added a sketch of the computer monitor to demonstrate some of the new brushes in Painter X.

Painter 11 Self-Portrait. I began with a photo, using Auto-Painting features, and then added someone else's lips and eye. Finishing touches include Image Hose sprays and Pattern Pen strokes.

Painter 12 Self-Portrait. No tricks were used here. This is a pastel portrait based on traditional techniques, with the photo serving only as a reference. Pastels at various sizes were used on tinted paper.

© 2014 Cengage Learning.

Portrait of Betsy. Several versions of a photo were created using filters from the Effects menu. Each of the versions was used as a clone source in the development of the painting.

Portrait of Hines. The photo is a composite of Hines and one of his abstract paintings. The center image is a digital painting based on the photo. The bottom image shows my 36" × 36" acrylic painting on canvas, inspired by the digital painting.

Portrait of Opa. This portrait from a photo relied on Cloner brushes as well as freehand pastel and pencil strokes on tinted paper.

Portrait: Semi-Automatic. This portrait was created from a photo, using several of the Auto-Painting features.

Character Design. Two poses for a character to be used in a video game.
The graffiti was created with an Airbrush variant and two brushes
from the F-X category: Fire and Fairy Dust.

© 2014 Cengage Learning.

Bob & Marlene on
Czech walking tour
of Pilsener beers

by Rhoda Draws 2011

Custom Postcard. Bob and Marlene wanted a custom caricature depicting a scene
of their trip to the Czech Republic.

View of Tiburon, CA. Based on a photo, this image uses pastel and pencil variants, with a variety of paper textures.

© 2014 Cengage Learning.

Loveseat Illustration. A variety of brushes and layer composite methods create a contemporary look for this leather sofa.

© 2014 Cengage Learning.

Index